Baseball Skills & Drills

American Baseball Coaches Association

ABCA

Mark Johnson
Texas A & M University

Jack Leggett
Clemson University

Pat McMahon
Mississippi State University

Project Coordinated by
John Winkin, Husson College

Human Kinetics

Library of Congress Cataloging-in-Publication Data

Baseball skills & drills / American Baseball Coaches Association ; John
Winkin . . . [et al.].
    p. cm.
    ISBN 0-7360-3738-1
    1. Baseball--Training. 2. Youth league baseball--Coaching. I. Title:
Baseball skills and drills. II. Winkin, John. III. American Baseball
Coaches Association.
    GV875.6 .B37 2001
    796.357'2--dc21

                                00-066981

ISBN-10: 0-7360-3738-1
ISBN-13: 978-0-7360-3738-9

Developmental Editor: Cynthia McEntire; **Assistant Editor:** Scott Hawkins; **Copyeditor:** Robert Replinger; **Proofreader:** Jim Burns; **Graphic Designer:** Robert Reuther; **Graphic Artist:** Kathleen Boudreau-Fuoss; **Photo Manager:** Clark Brooks; **Cover Designer:** Keith Blomberg; **Photographer (cover):** Tom Roberts; **Photographer (interior):** Tom Roberts unless otherwise noted; **Art Manager:** Craig Newsom; **Illustrator:** Sharon Smith; **Printer:** Versa Press

Human Kinetics books are available at special discounts for bulk purchase. Special editions or book excerpts can also be created to specification. For details, contact the Special Sales Manager at Human Kinetics.

Printed in the United States of America   15   14   13   12

Human Kinetics
Web site: www.HumanKinetics.com

United States: Human Kinetics, P.O. Box 5076, Champaign, IL 61825-5076
800-747-4457
e-mail: humank@hkusa.com

Canada: Human Kinetics, 475 Devonshire Road, Unit 100, Windsor, ON N8Y 2L5
800-465-7301 (in Canada only)
e-mail: orders@hkcanada.com

Europe: Human Kinetics, 107 Bradford Road, Stanningley
Leeds LS28 6AT, United Kingdom
+44 (0) 113 255 5665
e-mail: hk@hkeurope.com

Australia: Human Kinetics, 57A Price Avenue, Lower Mitcham, South Australia 5062
08 8372 0999
e-mail: liaw@hkaustralia.com

New Zealand: Human Kinetics, Division of Sports Distributors NZ Ltd.
P.O. Box 300 226 Albany, North Shore City, Auckland
0064 9 448 1207
e-mail: info@humankinetics.co.nz

Contents

PART III PITCHING AND CATCHING   151

Introduction

Coaching baseball for more than a half century has provided me a lifetime of lessons and memories. Teaching players of all backgrounds and abilities and seeing them develop to their full potential is one of the most satisfying experiences a coach can have. I certainly learned a lot along the way.

One enduring truth in baseball is that talent alone is no guarantee for success. Yes, so-called natural ability is a bonus for any athlete. But Hall of Famers and today's top players achieved greatness by combining their physical gifts with proper conditioning and frequent, repeated practicing of the game's essential skills—hitting, baserunning, pitching, catching, fielding, and throwing. Most players who excel take whatever talent they were blessed with and maximize their performance by working harder than their peers to master the fundamentals.

One of my former players at the University of Maine, Mike Bordick, typifies a player whose consistent execution of the basics made him an all-star. As he points out, baseball success doesn't happen by accident.

"I'm a firm believer in preparation, working at basic skills," Bordick said. "For me, that's the fun part. Some people, when they hear work, tend to shy away from it. But I love going down to the batting cage. I love taking ground balls. The most important thing is doing it all the right way." Amen.

Baseball Skills & Drills is for players and coaches who want to do it the right way, taking no shortcuts. The book covers the essential techniques, with three excellent coaches teaching the skills on which they are respected experts.

Offense by Mark Johnson

Defense by Jack Leggett

Pitching and Catching by Pat McMahon

In coordinating this project on behalf of the American Baseball Coaches Association, I had a hand in both selecting and working with these three men. All proved perfect choices, as they produced masterpieces on the development of fundamentals in their respective parts of the book.

Hitting a baseball is often considered the most difficult skill in any sport. Perhaps that is why there are so many approaches to teaching this aspect of the game. Whatever the approach, solid hitting is a result of two things—being quick with the bat and getting a good pitch to hit. Heavy-bat drills can improve quickness, but thousands of good at bats will be required to sharpen a player's sense of the strike zone.

Coach Johnson agrees with the "simpler is better" approach to hitting. His success in developing superb hitters attests to his extensive knowledge, straightforward teaching style, and at-the-plate practice regimen. As a believer in giving hitters lots of quality contact swings in practice, I find Mark's emphasis on doing it right and doing it often to be a sound and positive alternative to the hitting gimmicks that have crept into the modern game.

Behind every pitcher on a winning baseball team is a solid defense. When teams of mine did not make it into postseason play, what most often held them back was a failure to make the basic plays and double plays in the field. There is no such thing as the routine play. Unless players concentrate and use proper fundamentals on every play, lapses will occur.

Coach Jack Leggett's section on fielding is essential for any player who wants to contribute to his team with his glove and arm. It is filled with instructions and special teaching points on how to handle ground balls, line drives, and fly balls, and then make the correct throw. The many drills and fundamentals presented will enable players to field balls hit right at them, hit to the glove side, or hit to the throwing-arm side more effectively. Coach Leggett covers position-specific skills, relays, double plays, and many other fielding fundamentals.

Over the years, much has been written on pitching. I've read most of it. Nowhere has the topic been covered more succinctly or effectively than by Pat McMahon in chapters 11 through 17 in this book.

Coach McMahon teaches proper pitching technique, which is crucial in protecting the arm from injury. The pitching arm must explode toward the plate in synch with the body, neither too far ahead of it nor lagging behind it. Achieving the correct motion all hinges on being in balance and timing movements accurately through execution.

Effective pitch location is also stressed here, which, as Coach McMahon points out, is more important than pitch speed. Pitchers, especially young, developing pitchers, need to gain a sense of the strike zone and command of the ball to deliver it where they intend.

When Bill Swift arrived on our campus, he was primarily an outfielder who also happened to pitch. Once we convinced him that his future in the game was as a pitcher, he spent endless hours mastering the correct technique and focusing on proper pitch location. His hard work paid off as he led our team to the College World Series, pitched in the Olympics, and was a 20-game winner in the major leagues.

Baseball Skills & Drills is both a valuable learning tool for players and a teaching guide for coaches. The material in this book is not only authoritative from a technique instruction standpoint—it works! The success of the three coaches who wrote this book attests to the application of the content on the field. Make use of it in every practice session from now on and see the results.

John Winkin

Key to Diagrams

◯   Fielder throwing the ball initially to begin the play

▢   Relay man or cutoff man

- - - - - - - - -   Flight of the ball

△   Call man (calls where the ball should go)

⟶   Run path

▯   Tackle dummy

P   Pitcher

C   Catcher

CH   Coach

SS   Shortstop

1B   First baseman

2B   Second baseman

3B   Third baseman

B   Batter

R   Runner

LF   Left fielder

CF   Center fielder

RF   Right fielder

Drill Finder

PART I

Offense

How can you score runs without the help of the other team? To answer that question, you may picture a hitter in the batter's box crushing a "frozen rope." In some cases, that answers the question emphatically, but if you agree with the familiar maxim that "good pitching will beat good hitting," you must realize that the offensive side of baseball encompasses more than just hitting the ball.

Many have said that hitting a baseball may well be the most difficult task in all of athletics. The success ratio certainly bears witness to that statement. Rarely in any sport is 3 out of 10 considered successful, but that ratio is a mark of merit in hitting a baseball. Hitting is a difficult and often confusing task. We ask players to use a round bat to hit a round ball squarely.

Frank Sancet, the legendary former coach at the University of Arizona, once stated that 40 percent of the games a team wins aren't really won by the team—the other team loses them. Simply put, by making costly mistakes opponents will help you win games. But what do you do against a good team that won't help you win? A team like that is the one that shows up in the big games, the playoff games, and, yes, the championship games. The winning team must manufacture their own runs because their opponent plays solid defense and usually has an ace on the mound. Can you score runs with minimal hitting? If you have prepared well and have armed yourself with more than just a slugger, you have a chance.

Part I includes an in-depth discussion of hitting, of course, but it also covers other important areas that contribute to a successful offense. Teams that do not have high team batting averages still win championships! Such teams are usually highly skilled at bunting, baserunning, sliding, and situational hitting. The chapters in part I cover skills and drills on all aspects of offensive baseball.

So step up to the plate.

My section of this book is dedicated to all the coaches
that have graciously shared their baseball knowledge with me;
to my wife, Linda, who has supported my passion
for the game and who proofread my section;
and to Jason Hutchins who labored over my handwriting
and placed my thoughts in typewritten form.

Mark Johnson

Hitting

From the day that the baseball diamond was conceived and balls and bats were first gathered at the ballpark, the excitement and allure of hitting a baseball has been the central issue. The highlight of most practices and games for the individual player is usually associated with his turn at bat. The ground ball scooped and thrown to nip a runner at first, the fly ball snatched from going over the fence, the dust-churning slide safely into second, the curveball that catches the outside corner for strike three—these will almost always play second fiddle to the player's turn at bat. Ballplayers say it at practice every day: "Wait! Give me one more cut."

The art of hitting has been discussed, debated, practiced, filmed, studied, and analyzed since the game began. Rarely will you find two people who completely agree on all facets of hitting. Some fundamental conclusions, however, can give us a firm starting place for discussion:

1. If your hitting philosophies, ideas, and thoughts are based on sound mechanics, can accommodate individual idiosyncrasies, and if you believe in them, and can teach and sell them to your players, your ideas will have a good chance of working.

2. The better you are at teaching, the better your philosophy will work. It is not enough to have a sound idea of how to hit if you can't teach it to your players. This is indeed what separates the outstanding hitting instructor from the ineffective one. Knowledge is not enough. If you do not have a teaching method, the patience to teach, and the adaptability to work with every person individually to meet his needs, it will be difficult to reach and teach your players. This is one secret of being a good coach—reaching the players.

3. The better the hitter or athlete is, the better your philosophy will work. You may well have a sound philosophy, but you may not have a talented athlete to instruct. Although intangibles and exceptions can cloud the picture, most outstanding hitters have some special gifts and talents that allow them to succeed at this difficult task. A wise coach once said, "Leave the gifted, successful hitters alone. The ones you can help the most are the average talented hitters. You can make them good."

4. Remember that many of the best hitters ever to grace a ballpark were not and are not always solid in their mechanics. They simply had or have special talent to hit with what are perceived to be flaws for the normal hitter. But what they do works for them. What can we conclude? Simply that it is not always a good idea to base your instruction of hitting mechanics on a major leaguer who uses a hitch in his swing, wraps the bat as his hands move up, yet hits .300 and gets a 40-ounce bat through the hitting zone to knock a 93-mile-per-hour fastball 400 feet!

BASIC TEACHING APPROACH

The legendary former baseball coach at Clemson University, Bill Wilhelm, shares a poem that makes a lot of sense.

There once was a .400 hitter named Krantz,
who had a most unusual stance.
But with the coaches' correction
his stance is now perfection,
but he can't hit the seat of his pants.

Not all hitters hit alike—that would make it too easy! That's why they call hitting an art. The coach must be willing to let the hitter find his swing. A swing is like a signature. A person signs his name using the basic rudiments of the alphabet, but he uses his own unique handwriting. Each hitter has distinctive talents, gifts, and idiosyncrasies. The issue for improvement is to realize and identify the hitter's personal strengths and talents and, without restricting those areas, increase his competency.

One of the great authors of our time, Alex Haley, has a saying that he considers important: "Find the good and praise it." Perhaps we could add another phrase: "Find the good, praise it, and *build on it*." Praise is the foundation for improvement for all of us, certainly in hitting. It is proven every day that more success is attained because of praise and encouragement than by criticism and negativism.

Not only can we "find the good, praise it, and build on it" we can develop, enhance, and enlarge a hitter's self-image. All of us limit ourselves by setting boundaries about who we think we are and what we can achieve. As coaches, we have a unique opportunity to enhance a person's self-image by encouraging each player to believe he can achieve at a higher level. Self-image is critical in all phases of development and improvement. If a player feels good about himself, he will achieve at a higher rate. People who do not feel good about themselves rarely accomplish great things. Helping others feel good about themselves is part of parenting, teaching, and coaching. It is part of helping others to rise to the next level.

Perhaps the most important skill in coaching is to be able to teach with a variety of terminologies that can establish a positive mental picture, or proper visualization. If a hitter cannot picture in his mind the mechanics you are teaching, he will not be able to produce the intended results. Not all hitters will respond with the same visual mental picture to a simple comment. Telling a hitter who is dipping his back shoulder to "stay tall on the back side" may mean absolutely nothing. He simply cannot picture it. But asking him to keep his front shoulder lower than his back shoulder may give him the intended result. Physical skills require mental pictures. The mind must see to achieve. The body will respond to the mind's picture. If the picture is a result of a negative instruction, the outcome will usually be negative. For example, the instruction "Don't drop your back shoulder" will usually produce a dropped back shoulder because that is the picture. Teach with positive mental pictures and your results will have a better chance of reaching fruition.

GENERAL HITTING PHILOSOPHY

An old farmer once said to a lost motorist who happened upon his farmhouse, "If you don't know where you are going, any road will get you there." Players too often learn hitting techniques without understanding the results they wish to accomplish. Does the hitter want to try to hit home runs all the time? Does he want to take a lot of pitches? Does he just want to hit the ball to the opposite side? If a player is to be a successful hitter, he must have a philosophy.

A solid hitting philosophy includes five basic elements:

1. The longer the hitter can wait, the better hitter he will be.

2. Line drives and ground balls win games.

3. The hitter should have a plan at the plate.

4. The hitter should understand the three Ps—patience, persistence, and poise.

5. Drills and fundamentals are important.

The Longer the Hitter Can Wait, the Better Hitter He Will Be

This statement refers to the hitter's ability to identify the pitch and location before committing to a forward movement of his swing. Research indicates it takes an 80-mile-per-hour pitch approximately four-tenths of a second to travel to home plate. Research also tells us that the hitter requires two-tenths of a second to read the pitch properly. Thus the hitter has two-tenths of a second to deliver the blow to the ball with the bat. Herein lies the centerpiece, the core, the pure essence, of hitting. Most of the problems in hitting a baseball are caused by starting the swing too early, before getting a good read on the ball. Hitters who start too early are fooled on curveballs, change-ups, and pitch location. Their timing is off on the swing.

If we agree that the early start is the initial culprit of most problems in hitting, then why don't hitters wait longer to initiate the forward movement of the swing? There are probably hundreds of reasons why this occurs. Here are a few worth mentioning. (It may be worth noting that this inquiry approach may be a good teaching method: here is the objective, here is the problem. Before correcting a problem, let's find out why we have the problem. This method gives us a better chance to solve the puzzle.)

1. The hitter has flaws in his swing and requires more than two-tenths of a second to get the bat to the ball.

2. The hitter is not strong enough or quick enough to get the bat to the ball in the allotted time for success. Perhaps the bat is too heavy.

3. The hitter believes the age-old misconception that has tempted every hitter: if I take a long, hard, powerful swing at the ball, it will go farther, perhaps even over the fence. Every hitter would like to hit home runs. In an attempt to do so, he creates a long swing that requires an early start.

4. The hitter brings anxiety to the plate, which creates poor focus. He is not playing in the now, in the moment. He brings garbage to the plate. His concentration is poor, and he doesn't properly pick up the ball as the pitcher releases it. He starts early.

5. The hitter lacks confidence in his ability to hit. He simply does not trust his stuff. He starts early.

6. The hitter tries to guess every pitch rather than read the pitch. This is a dangerous trap because the hitter will eventually reach a level of play in which the pitcher's arsenal is so varied that he will be unable to guess correctly. Because most hitters guess fastballs or pitches in, they start early.

7. The hitter refuses to get beat on the inside fastball; thus his approach to the swing starts early so that he can get the bat head out in front to meet the inside pitch. Getting beat inside with the bat means a possible broken bat, a weak ground ball, or what is referred to as "bees,"—a sting of the hands. Although the results are

not as damaging with the aluminum bat, the desire to win the battle inside continues. This has always has been the contest, and it always will be. For most hitters, proper contact on the inside pitch will produce a harder hit ball, which increases the chance for a home run. The striving for a home run creeps back in! Most hitters do not have opposite-side power; thus they must sit on the inside pitch. The origin of this problem is twofold: a hitter has a major goal of hitting home runs, and his ego, his manliness, will take precedence over using proper hitting style. Simply put, making outs or poor contact on pitches away from him does not bother him nearly as much as getting jammed and beat on an inside pitch. To be a good hitter, this thinking must be addressed and adjusted because most outs and most pitches occur on the outer half of the plate. Players must move their competitive nature to the next level and learn to play smart baseball.

Other reasons could be the cause for the early start, but those just listed are the most common. Solid observation of the good hitters, the major-league hitters, shows many more late swings or foul balls to the opposite side than early swings or foul balls to the pull side. At lower levels of expertise, we observe the opposite result.

If we are to accept the philosophy that the longer the hitter can wait, the better the hitter he will be, then proper adjustments—physically, emotionally, and mentally—must occur. The hitter must develop a short, compact stroke. He must keep his power base intact throughout the swing. This means that the ankles and knees do not travel beyond his feet as he shifts back and transfers forward. He must adhere to the rule of transferring his weight from back to middle, not from back to front.

Line Drives and Ground Balls Win Games

Year-in and year-out, a larger percentage of games will be won by the team with the highest on-base average rather than the team with the highest slugging percentage. Another truism is that a swing that produces line drives and ground balls takes less time than one that hits fly balls. This correlates with our first premise: the hitter must find a swing that does not require an early start.

Many studies have been conducted concerning productivity of ground balls, fly balls, and line drives. Most studies at the NCAA Division I level conclude:

1. For every 10 ground balls hit, 3 will fall in for base hits. On-base average results are 42 percent.
2. For every 10 line drives hit, 8 will fall in for base hits. On-base average results are 84 percent.
3. For every 10 fly balls hit (including all home runs), 2 will fall in for base hits. On-base average results are 29 percent.

Keep in mind that these statistics are for top amateur baseball players playing against highly skilled defenses on playing surfaces that are usually better than other amateur fields. We could certainly argue that batting averages and on-base averages would increase with less-skilled defenses or poorly manicured fields. More base hits would occur on fly balls, but the increase for ground balls and line drives would be even greater. It is simply easier to catch a fly ball than it is to stop a ground ball, throw it accurately to a base, and have a teammate catch it.

Likewise, line drives are harder to catch than fly balls; defenses can run down fly balls more easily than they can line drives.

In summary, if you believe on-base average wins more games, then line drives and ground balls are the route to take.

Have a Plan at the Plate

As a reference point to ensure understanding, hitters should normally (a) hit the inside pitch to the pull side, (b) hit the outside pitch to the opposite side, and (c) hit the pitch down the middle to the middle of the field. This is an absolute in hitting. Successful hitters rarely deviate from this absolute, although we can find some exceptions among outstanding hitters.

Unless a hitter is in a guess count (3-1, 2-0), his initial thought is to work from a plan that the next pitch will be in the middle of the plate and high in the strike zone. His mental plan will be to hit a line drive up the middle. Although plans do not always work out, the hitter using this plan can more easily make adjustments as the pitch is thrown. If we say that the middle of the plate is five inches wide, then we must adjust to around six inches for the outer half of the plate and six inches for the inner half. In reality, most hitters, either consciously or unconsciously, work from the premise that the pitch will be more toward the inside. This, of course, goes back to our earlier comment concerning the battle of not getting beat inside. Obviously, in expecting the pitch inside, the hitter must make greater adjustments to the outside pitch in the strike zone, adjustments that are often unsuccessful. In like manner, the hitter will hit fewer pop-ups or foul balls if he has a basic starting plan on a ball up in the zone. It is much easier to adjust down than adjust up, and the results are normally more productive.

Successful hitting requires aggressiveness. The pitcher starts the action; he throws the first blow. The hitter must be prepared to respond aggressively. Aggressiveness will overcome many flaws in a swing.

As stated earlier, the hitter has a short amount of time to decide to swing. A good, aggressive hitter has already made half of that decision when he approaches the plate. Rather than making two decisions, either to swing or not to swing, the aggressive hitter makes only one decision—not to swing. He goes to the plate already planning to swing.

Good hitters primarily use the middle of the field. That is, the balls they hit will travel between the shortstop and second baseman or to the power alleys in the outfield. Again, we can note exceptions, but we find that the hitters with high batting averages do not consistently pull or consistently push. Pitchers have a much easier time beating the pull hitter or push hitter. The tough ones are those who consistently use the middle of the field.

Few hitters, even good hitters, can control both sides of the plate. It simply is too wide an area. Thus they must choose. Most will pick the inside area to just past the midway point of the plate. Unless the hitter is exceptional, this is a poor choice. When we chart and study pitchers, particularly in amateur baseball, we notice that over 70 percent of the pitches in the strike zone are from just inside the midway point of the plate to the outside corner. Many more outs are made on the outside half of the plate. A wise choice when learning to control the width of the plate is to choose an area a little inside the midway point of the plate and toward the outside corner.

The hitter trying to increase the area of the plate that he can control should work from the area he can control toward his poorly controlled area. If he can control the outside half of the plate and wants to enlarge his skill at controlling more of the plate, he does not go to the inside corner. He works on increasing his control from the middle of the plate slightly toward the inner half.

The good hitter will tell you that RBI hits are usually in the middle of the field or to the opposite side. With a runner in scoring position, most pitchers will work the outer half of the plate with fastballs, curveballs, or sliders because that is where they can get the outs. Obviously, we are talking percentage baseball here, but this trend has been around since the game began.

As long as we are mentioning percentage baseball, we must also mention that with few exceptions, the fastball is an easier pitch to hit than the breaking ball. The hitter is wise to make an effort to hit a fastball. Ralph Garr, a former major leaguer who has held many of the Atlanta Braves' offensive records, once made a statement that relates to this premise concerning the fastball: "The best way to hit the curveball is not to miss the fastball!" He made every effort to hit the fastball because he knew he could hit it better than he could the curveball. Early in the count, it is wise to give away both corners of the plate (two to three inches on both sides) and look for a fastball to hit to the middle of the field. Many good hitters make a living doing just that. The hitter can't win every at bat, but he can put the percentages in his favor.

We've discussed some of the thinking that players might use on the walk from the on-deck circle to the batter's box. Having a plan and putting it in a mental picture, visualizing the plan, is critical. But the hitter has no time to think and hit once the ball is released. He must be relaxed and focused enough to let reflexes take over in the mental picture that he has established. Thinking and having a high-percentage plan is critical, and the hitter must rehearse it in mental pictures. He visualizes his plan, his swing, and where the ball will go. If the player wants success, he must first visualize it.

Understand the Three Ps

Successful people exhibit many distinctive traits. The three Ps—patience, persistence, and poise—are normally present in all types of successful people, including successful hitters.

Patience. It has been said that "good things take time." Certainly, this holds true in hitting. Hours, days, months, and years of practice are required to develop from a 2-for-10 hitter to a 3-for-10 hitter. As in all journeys to excellence, the road is not straight or smooth. The bumps and curves in the road are discouraging and require patience. Nobody will reach success in hitting in a short time. An education professor once mentioned, "Yard by yard it's hard, but inch by inch it's a cinch!" The hitter must address and learn all parts of the swing. A hitter can't learn them all at the same time. A good phrase to keep in mind might be, "In some small way I can improve on yesterday today." The hitter must be patient and persistent.

Persistence. Patience and persistence have some overlap, but persistence has a more aggressive tone. All of us have a 24-hour day. No one has more and no one has less. How we use those 24 hours each day will determine who we are and who we will become.

If a person wants to be a good hitter, he must, as the old coach once said, "Just keep on, keeping on." It may take one hundred and one knocks on the door before it opens, but he who knocks that last time will be glad he did not stop at one hundred. If a player wants to become a good hitter, he must work harder than most others do. It will take more than the six to eight cuts that he gets at practice. He must be willing to hit off the tee or hit soft tosses thrown by a friend, Dad, or Mom in the backyard using a tied-up old rag. Good hitters find a way to swing the bat. Success seldom happens by accident.

Poise. As in any journey toward excellence, the bumps on the road can cause frustration. If a player wants to be a good hitter, he must develop resiliency, or poise, because he will experience more failure than success. Hitting is one of the few activities in which a standard of excellence is defined by failing 70 percent of the time. That's right—a .300 hitter is successful only 3 times out of 10. Each at bat is a new at bat, and the hitter must be able to forget the previous one. The 70 percent ratio of failure has often caused a good hitter to become average because he lacks poise. If a hitter is 0 for 3 and has a chance to drive in the winning run in the last inning, he can't carry the 0 for 3 to the plate and call it a bad day. The hitter with poise believes that the percentage is in his favor to drive in that run. Remember, each moment of our lives is influenced by the previous moment. The hitter must maintain his poise and think positively.

Drills and Fundamentals Are Important

Achievement in all areas of expertise requires learning fundamental principles or skills. If a player does not learn the fundamentals of hitting, improvement will come slowly and, in most cases, only because of maturation. The hitter will eventually reach a level where he can advance no further. It is that simple, and it is proven every day at the ballfield. Fundamentals must be taught and learned.

The progression of learning the fundamentals is often more successful when the fundamentals are broken down into parts and then placed back together into the entire fundamental. Later in this chapter, we will address these fundamentals individually and introduce drills to reinforce each hitting skill. Another advantage of isolating parts of the hitting skill in drills is that the hitter eventually will feel that particular skill and realize its existence. Thus he will be able to make proper adjustments to his swing when things are not going well.

Although we know it is not possible for every hitter to get 120 live, pitched balls to hit every day, it is possible to get 120 cuts each day by implementing drills such as tee work, short toss, or soft toss. If repetition is the father of learning, then we must find areas to get the cuts in.

STANCE

Every ballplayer has a unique stance. What is the perfect stance? It is the one that is right for the hitter! The stance must be comfortable and allow the hitter to attain a launch position without causing imbalance or restricting vision. It must be a body position that allows the uniqueness in the swing to deliver the blow.

a   b

Figure 1.1   The basic stance.

a   b   c

Figure 1.2   (a) Normal stance; (b) closed stance; (c) open stance.

For the purpose of this book, let's present a stance that can be a starting place from which each hitter can grow into his own, special stance. Figure 1.1 shows two views of a basic stance.

Lower Body

The normal stance has both feet in proper alignment. That is, if the batter laid a bat on the ground that touched the big toes of both feet, it would point directly to the

Checklist for the Stance

- Feet are slightly wider than shoulder-width.
- Weight is on the balls of the feet.
- The back foot is pointed slightly in (pigeon-toed).
- The knees are slightly bent.
- The waist is bent slightly forward.
- The shoulders are level, or the front shoulder is down slightly.
- The front arm is down with the elbow bent at a 90-degree angle.
- The back elbow is down.
- The bat is more flat than straight up and points in a path from the hands to the top of the back shoulder.
- The hands are six to eight inches away from the back shoulder and at the top of the strike zone.
- The head is straight up; the hitter should be able to see the pitcher with his front eye closed.
- The body is properly stacked, one part on top of the next part in balance.

mound (figure 1.2a). The player may choose to deviate a little. In the closed stance, the bat would point toward the hitter's opposite side (figure 1.2b); in the open stance, the bat would point toward his pull side (figure 1.2c).

The big toe of the back foot should face in slightly, toward the front foot in a pigeon-toed appearance. This positioning allows two things to happen:

1. In most cases, it will ensure that the player's weight will be on the balls of the feet just in front of the insteps.
2. An easier rotation of the back knee and hip will occur as the body rotates toward the area where the hitter wishes to send the ball.

The front foot should point straight ahead or be slightly closed, or pigeon-toed. This positioning will help keep the front side of the body from opening early.

The weight of the body should be on the balls of the feet (not the toes and certainly not the heels). Approximately 60 percent of the body weight should be on the back foot. This distribution will vary depending on how the hitter shifts into the launch position, but it is a good starting place.

The distance between the feet should be a little wider than shoulder-width. This placement normally allows for the desired shorter stride.

The knees should be slightly bent and slightly inside the width of the feet. The player normally attains this positioning simply by placing the body weight on the balls of the feet.

The hitter should bend slightly at the waist to keep his stance from being too rigid. But he should not bend forward to a point where each body part is not properly stacked on top of the other (knees above the feet, chest above the knees, head above the chest).

Upper Body

In the normal stance, the shoulders should be in straight alignment to the mound, although they may close slightly as the hitter moves to his launch position. The shoulders should be parallel to the ground, or the front shoulder can be slightly lower than the back shoulder. In no case should the back shoulder be lower than the front shoulder.

The hitter's grip on the bat depends on the size of his hands in relation to the size of the bat handle. Most batters should grip the bat with the calloused areas where the fingers join the hands. This somewhat aligns the middle knuckles of each hand and allows the hands and fingers to be involved in the final summation of forces as the bat head is thrust toward the ball. If the hitter has small hands, his bottom hand should hold the bat in the meat of the hand, and the top hand should hold the bat along the calloused area where the fingers and hand meet.

The hitter should hold the bat at approximately the height of the strike zone six to eight inches in front of his back shoulder or armpit. The bat should be almost parallel to the ground. This bat positioning is called a *flat bat*. The bat is a few inches above the back shoulder. An excellent tip is simply to rest the bat on the back shoulder in the stance. Although this is not comfortable to most hitters, it does provide a common touch point and places the bat in a proper position to hit.

Some hitters prefer to have the bat pointing more toward the sky. In most cases this means that the player must drop the bat into the flat position before it travels toward the contact area with the ball. This motion often causes mechanical problems, and it requires a longer path to the ball. If the hitter does not flatten the bat, the swing then becomes like a golf swing and is not conducive to hitting a pitch up or in the strike zone. Many strong athletes succeed with this bat positioning, but the normal hitter should have a flat bat stance.

The elbow of the front arm should be bent at approximately 90 degrees and in a down position. The elbow of the back arm should also be in a down position, although it can be slightly higher than the front elbow. Many coaches teach a high back elbow so that the swing will produce fewer fly balls and more ground balls. Although this positioning usually works, it is not because of the high back elbow. It is a result of the front shoulder dropping down when the back elbow is raised. A hitter can and should keep the front shoulder down without raising the back elbow. He must drop a high back elbow as the swing begins, which takes time and can cause a late bat.

The head positioning is often omitted from the discussion of a proper stance. But this area is critical to achieving proper vision, balance, and swing.

The hitter must turn the head sufficiently toward the pitcher so that both eyes can properly read the pitch. The hitter should retain this vision even after he moves into launch position. Occasionally, a player will get in his stance or launch position and not realize that his vision is impaired because he can see the ball with only his front eye. Players with closed stances are especially susceptible to this problem. Have the player get in his stance, close his front eye, and then move to his launch position. If he loses sight of the pitcher in either position, he must make adjustments.

The hitter attains the best vision when his head is straight up. The more tilted the head becomes, the poorer the vision will be. Watching television while lying on the couch with your head on a pillow will not provide a good perspective of the action on the screen. If you want good vision, you must sit up with your head straight up. Likewise, a hitter should always hold his head upright when trying to hit.

Although head position influences vision, improper head position can cause two additional problems. At the top of the pyramid, with each part stacked onto another, a head tilt can cause an imbalance that the hitter must adjust for lower in the stance. An equal and opposite response must occur. This may mean placing too much weight on the heels or moving the buttocks away from the plate. The body must remain properly stacked for optimum results to occur.

Finally, the head tilt can control the path of the bat to the ball. A strong correlation exists between the head tilt and the slice swing—a swing that resembles a golf swing in which the hitter casts the bat head back away from the ball and drops it below the hands too early in the swing. To analyze this problem, the batter can imagine himself with an exaggerated head tilt and then visualize the possibility of swinging a bat parallel to the ground. Accomplishing this is difficult and awkward. Thus, for a level swing, the head should remain in the stack.

SWING

We have built up to this moment. The hitter has established a philosophy, and he knows what his objective is. He understands the mental, emotional, and visual parts of hitting, and he has placed himself in a good, solid stance. He is ready to reduce the game from a team game to a one-on-one-battle between himself and the pitcher. He must be ready to respond. The strike zone belongs to him!

For a point of clarification concerning our terminology and objective, we must define two areas before starting our discussion of the swing.

1. Imagine a straight line splitting the body from nose to belly button to a point between the feet. All parts of the body closest to the pitcher make up the *front side;* the parts farthest from the pitcher make up the *back side.*

2. Understand the basic law in the power skills of our sport, throwing and hitting. The player stays behind the final summation of the forces he is trying to generate until he reaches the final stages of the release of energy. He does not leak, jump, lunge, shift, or transfer weight before that time. This is a universal problem in both power skills. It is why we tell hitters to "stay back" and use the term "rushing" with pitchers. The hitter transfers his weight in front of the bat when hitting, or the pitcher transfers his weight in front of his hand and arm when throwing. When this happens, the power side (the back side) loses its force, creating a slow bat or a sweeping swing or, in throwing, a slow, slinging arm action.

Cock, or Load, Position

The cock, or load, is the movement back to the launch position. The launch position is the point in the swing where the player generates all movement forward to hit the ball.

To establish proper rhythm and timing, most activities in athletics require a movement back before a movement forward. The boxer pulls his fist back before striking forward; the golfer moves the club back before going forward; the tennis player moves the racket back before going forward; the pitcher goes back before going forward; and the hitter goes back before going forward. This action is referred to as the load, or the cock of the gun, for the hitter.

The load goes before the stride! A separation, however small, must occur between the load and the stride. When the two happen simultaneously, the lower half of the body goes forward and the upper half goes backward. If no separation occurs, a hitter will rarely reach his potential.

The load should occur just as the pitcher is preparing to release the ball. It should be a smooth, comfortable movement that brings rhythm to the swing. Timing is critical. Rhythm is destroyed if the load ends and a long pause occurs before the swing starts.

We should understand that almost every athlete will instinctively move somehow before the swing. What he does in this simple, instinctive movement can destroy his swing or prepare him to have a great swing. Here is where you see players hitch, wrap the bat around the head, straighten the front arm, or perform other actions that will hinder the timing and the swing. The load must smoothly place the bat in the proper launch position.

The load is a movement back (figure 1.3). A slight inward rotational movement can occur in the front-side hip or shoulder. The front knee should make a small inward turn, and the hands should go back slightly. The front arm must retain its 90-degree angle. If the front arm straightens out, the hitter has just created a longer

Figure 1.3 The load position is a simple movement back.

Checklist for the Load

- The front knee is slightly in.
- A little more weight (maybe 10 percent) has been transferred to the inside of the ball of the back foot.
- The back knee is still above or inside the back foot.
- The shoulders can rotate slightly inward.
- The front arm goes back slightly but remains close to a 90-degree angle at the elbow.
- The bat remains close to its original position. The bat head does not wrap around the player's head; that movement significantly increases the distance the bat must travel to get to the ball.
- The hands move back slightly but do not drop below their original position in the stance. When they drop, the motion is what we call a hitch, which often causes a late swing.
- At the completion of the load, the player should be able to shut his front eye and still see the pitcher.

lever arm, which requires more time to swing. The idea is to remain flexed. "From flexion to extension" is a term we need to remember. The hitter must reach the launch position with the arms flexed so that he can get extension at contact with the ball.

A small weight shift back is permissible. If 60 percent of the hitter's weight is on his back foot in the stance, he can bring another 10 percent back. Be sure that this weight transfer does not cause the back knee to travel past the back foot. The weight should remain toward the inside of the back foot. The knees should always be slightly inside the feet throughout the swing.

Stride

"If the load doesn't get you, the stride will." This statement refers to two major problem areas for hitters. Regardless of the player's talent, he can learn to execute the load and the stride properly. The hitter then has a solid foundation on which to let his God-given talents take over.

The stride occurs as the pitch is delivered. Again, it should follow immediately after the load has reached the launch position.

The stride should be short (six to eight inches), in the direction of the pitcher, and without significant weight transfer. The idea is to step softly as though stepping on thin ice. Any weight transferred should remain on the inside of the striding foot toward the big toe. Again, to produce a short, compact, quick stroke, the stride must be no longer than eight inches.

A couple of sayings are worth mentioning here:

1. "The longer the stride, the poorer the hitter." A long stride causes an early weight transfer, breaking the rule of staying behind the final summation of forces

Checklist for the Stride

- The stride is short (six to eight inches) and toward the pitcher.
- The stride is a soft step that takes little transfer of weight from the back foot.
- The stride lands on the big toe.
- The head travels forward no more than one or two inches.
- The hands remain in the load position. A hitter will often let the hands leak forward, reducing his power.
- Check the stack. Is it balanced? Many hitters lean forward at the waist toward the plate. Some let their buttocks move back away from the plate (sitting); this shifts the weight to the heels. The stack must be aligned.

(the hands and bat). A long stride separates the knees, and the farther the knees are separated, the longer it takes to swing the bat. Bat-speed tests have proven that the shorter the distance between the two elbows and the two knees, the faster the bat will travel.

2. "Length of stride dictates length of stroke." If the stride is long, the swing will also likely be long. Imagine taking a long stride and using a very short stroke, or taking a short stride, driving the back knee toward the front knee, and swinging in a long bat path. A long stride and a short swing, or a short stride and a long swing, just don't match.

As the hitter completes the stride, the hands and bat should still be back. They do not leak forward with the stride. Ultimately, the head should travel no more than one or two inches with the stride. Once the front foot hits the ground, the head should remain still throughout the swing. To test the stride, have the hitter get a fungo bat or stick that will rest comfortably under his buttocks. He holds it straight, perpendicular to the ground as though he were sitting on it. He takes his stride. If the bat or stick moves toward the pitcher off its upward line more than two or three inches, he is overstriding or transferring too much weight.

The hitter should keep the stride short and soft.

Launch Position

A proper load should place the hitter in position to launch his energy forward. The stride should not interrupt the launch position. Approximately 65 percent of the weight should be back and on the inside of the back foot. The back knee should be slightly inside the back foot. The hands should be back at the top of the strike zone within six to eight inches of the shoulder. The front elbow should be down and at a 90-degree angle. The back elbow will rise slightly but should not be close to shoulder height. The front shoulder should be even with or lower than the back shoulder. The head should be straight up, and the stack should be in balance (feet, knees, waist, chest, and head in upward, balanced alignment). The hitter should be sure the front foot and front side are not open toward the pitcher.

The moment to hit has arrived. All movements before this time should be comfortable, effortless, and rhythmical. The hitter should use no force to create the load or the stride.

Rotation Forward

Just as the load and stride follow each other in sequence, so does the forceful movement forward to strike the ball (figure 1.4).

The movement starts from the ground up. The feet must be firmly planted on the ground. The hips start the swing, getting the stronger muscles in the body, the legs, involved. To rotate the back hip forward, the hitter pivots on the ball of the back foot. Remember, the stance began with the back foot pointed slightly in, which allows for a quicker pivot. An analogy may help the player learn this pivot. Ask the player to pretend that he has stepped on a bug with the ball of his back foot. The bug is in soft dirt, so he is undamaged but trapped. Now, if the hitter transfers his weight early or overstrides, the heel of the back foot will move upward so that only the toes are touching the ground. The bug can escape if this happens. The hitter must keep him trapped. The objective is to squash the bug by pivoting the foot forward with the weight staying directly over the ball of the foot where the bug is trapped.

Checklist for Hip Rotation

- The hips rotate farther on an inside pitch than on an outside pitch. Wherever the pitch is located, the back knee and belly button should face the direction the ball will travel off the bat at the conclusion of the swing.
- The hips rotate on a level plane. Check the hitter's waistband or belt. If the front side is higher than the back side, the back knee collapsed too much. Judge the bat in the same manner.
- The hip rotation is released by the pivot, or the squash of the bug, on the ball of the back foot. If the back foot does not rotate, the hitter will not have good hip rotation or proper balance.
- The hitter retains body balance throughout the rotation. Often the weight falls toward the plate because of a poor pivot on the back side or a weight transfer outside the stack.
- The weight transfer is from back to middle. The back foot remains in solid contact with the ground. The hitter must not let the bug escape before he squashes it!
- A bracing off of the front knee occurs on imaginary contact with the ball.
- The hitter feels himself drive the front hip out of the way. The front hip does not pull the back hip forward.

Figure 1.4 The swing: (a) the rotation begins; (b) hip rotation; (c) brace off; (d) putting the ball in play.

Remember that we talked about rotating the back hip forward. Note that the front hip does not pull the back hip forward. Power will come from the back side. The back hip must drive the front hip out. Remember also that the goal is a level swing. The hips must rotate on a level plane. The back hip must not drop below the front hip. If that occurs, the hitter will have an upward swing that produces fly balls. An upward swing is often caused by bending the back knee so far that it collapses and causes the back hip to drop below the front hip.

The hitter must keep the hips over the feet and keep the stack in order. He does not sit, that is, he does not move his hips away from the plate or behind the feet. That sort of movement shifts the weight to the heels, alters the stack, and causes loss of power. The pivot cannot be properly executed with the weight on the heels.

The hip rotation must not extend past the place where the bat will hit the ball. If it does, the force of the hips pulls energy away from maximum force on the ball. This action is called *spinning*. When the bat makes contact with the ball, the back knee and belly button should face the area to which the batter is hitting the ball. If he hits the ball to the opposite side, the rotation will not be as great as it will be if he pulls the ball. Rotation is directly related to the location of the pitch. An inside pitch is hit farther in front of the plate than the outside pitch; thus the inside pitch requires more rotation than the outside pitch.

Let's slow down for a minute and contemplate what we have just said because it is a point that separates good hitters from average hitters. Many hitters start rotation and weight transfer when they read velocity but not location. And, of course, most of the time they rotate and shift weight to hit a pitch thrown toward the inside of the plate. It is amazing how often the battle to win inside comes up! Consequently, these hitters are stuck adjusting to the outside pitch too far in front of the plate, and they lose their power base. Their adjustment, if any, is to push the ball weakly to the opposite side, normally with the bat head dragging below the hands. Pop-ups usually result. If the hitter makes no adjustment in this early transfer, he usually pulls the ball weakly off the end of the bat. Remember, the swing should always have the same approach. The big decision is where to make contact with the ball in relation to its flight to the strike zone. The inside pitch must be hit farther in front of the plate than the outside pitch.

Shoulder Rotation

Obviously, the hip rotation will be followed in sequence by the abdomen, chest, and shoulders. These areas will move naturally in response to what the hips are doing. Note that the front-side shoulder, like the front-side hip, will stay closed until the back shoulder forces it out. If the front shoulder is the force, it will drag the back shoulder forward. This action will not provide a quick, forceful swing. The hitter should use the front shoulder to point toward the ball until the back shoulder comes forward. If the hips are rotating on a level plane, it follows that the shoulders will rotate on a level plane. Any sequence in movement that rotates at a different angle than the previous motion will disrupt the generation of force, which will reduce power and quickness.

Weight Transfer

The movement of weight from the back foot begins after the pivot starts. The hitter can keep in mind several notions or pictures concerning weight transfer.

First, he must keep the power base in order. He simply does not allow the weight to transfer so much that he loses his solid base with the back foot. He should remember that he is squashing a bug. The ball of the back foot must remain solidly on the ground. If the back foot comes off the ground or drags forward as the hitter makes contact, he has shifted too much weight and lost the power base. The power base stays in balance throughout the swing. This means that the knees and body weight stay inside the base (feet).

Second, weight transfer should move from the back to the middle of the body; it should not move from back to front. The hitter should remember the fungo or stick that he used to check his stride. He can imagine that stick going through his body to the tip of his head and remaining perpendicular to the ground. Transferring from back to front would not only cause the stick to lose its perpendicular line but also break the rule of allowing the head to transfer after the stride is complete. The hitter goes from back to middle in weight shift.

Brace Off

To involve centrifugal force in the swing, the front knee should momentarily straighten as the hitter generates maximum bat speed at contact with the ball. To apply centrifugal force, a bracing off must occur. If the weight shifts forward too much, the front knee will be outside the front foot and a bracing off will not occur. Hitters who are successful without a bracing off are normally extremely strong in the arms and the hands.

Bat Arc

If the hitter has rotated the body in proper sequence and the forward direction of force from the knees to the hips to the shoulder is in a level plane to the ground, the bat arc should be in the same plane, that is, a level swing should occur. If this happens, if all forces are rotating in the same plane, the hitter has a good chance to apply his optimum force to the ball. How he approaches the ball becomes critical at this point. The following rules concern the approach to the ball.

The hands always should stay higher than the path of the ball as the hitter approaches the ball. He must not drop the hands to the path of the ball as he begins his approach. Doing so takes time, causes fly balls, and reduces power and quickness.

The hands should stay inside the path of the ball, close to the power stance. The farther the hands are from the body, the longer, slower, and weaker the swing will be. If the hitter holds the hands away from the body, contact will often occur on the outside of the ball, resulting in a hooking spin that will reduce the distance that the ball will travel. Ultimately, the hitter wants to hit directly behind the ball toward the area he is aiming for. If he misses, it is far better to miss by hitting the inside of the ball rather than the outside of the ball. A good rule is simply to take the knob of the bat to the ball and lead the swing with the hands, not the barrel of the bat. This action will produce a quicker bat, offer a better chance of reading the pitch before starting the swing, and allow a proper path to the pitch on the outer half of the plate.

In the initial approach to the ball, the barrel of the bat remains higher than the hands, and the hands remain higher than the front elbow. Two major problems cause hitters to break this rule:

1. The back shoulder dips below the level of the front shoulder because the back knee and hip collapse or because the hitter simply dips the back shoulder. This causes

the plane of the bat arc to become longer as the hitter casts the bat away from the flight of the ball. The barrel quickly becomes lower than the hands and the front elbow. The barrel then moves in an upward arc, which will disrupt the force plane if the knees and hips have maintained a rotation parallel to the ground. The longer approach results in an upward swing and fly balls that generate a low on-base percentage.

2. The front elbow moves upward. The hitter breaks the rule of keeping his elbow lower than his hands and the barrel of the bat. The result is a long, golf-like swing that requires great accuracy in timing as it reaches the point of contact with the ball. The timing must be perfect to hit line drives because the bat is not traveling in the same plane as the ball. In a manner similar to what happens when the hitter dips the back shoulder, the bat arc is in a completely different plane from hip rotation. The hitter loses power. Again, the bat is cast away from the flight of the ball, and the swing takes longer. This slicing at the ball leaves holes in the swing areas in the strike zone, usually up and in where the hitter has a poor chance of making good contact. In addition, the golflike swing is extremely difficult to adjust to pitches that have lateral movement (in or away, not up or down), as most do.

Obviously, the bat gets lower than the hands as it contacts the ball on the low pitch, but on the initial approach, the barrel of the bat must remain higher than the hands to produce a solid, quick bat that goes straight to the ball.

Straight to the Ball

Obviously, the quickest path between two points is a straight line. In hitting, the two points are the ball and the barrel of the bat. From launch position, the barrel must take a straight path to the ball. It cannot be cast back away from the ball. It cannot go down in a curved path to the ball. It must go straight to the path of the ball. To the novice it would seem that this somewhat downward approach to the ball would result in beating the ball into the ground. All we are trying to do is reach the path of the ball quickly. Upon reaching that path, the hitter levels off and follows through, ideally with the bat touching the top of the front arm. If the follow-through takes the hands to the front knee, then, yes, the hitter would be beating the ball in the ground.

Swings that conclude with the hands well above the front shoulder normally have an upward bat path, again resulting in fly balls. The hands should finish at the top of the front-side arm. That ending position indicates a level swing that is in concert with the rotational forces.

Generating Bat Speed

The hitter should generate optimum bat speed as the bat makes contact with the ball, not after contact. He should center his thoughts on generating bat speed from launch position to the ball. The back side must generate power.

Fighting for Extension

The front elbow should never be fully extended, but the back elbow should be close to full extension at contact with the ball. Before that time, the front elbow should be flexed so that the lever arm is short and can be moved more quickly. Imagine the difference between swinging a long broom handle and a short broom handle. The shorter handle will always move more quickly. The longer broom handle may generate more power, but it may not get to the ball in time.

As the hitter reaches extension, the bat arc should go through the ball. The swing is not a perfect circle. As the body rotates and bracing off occurs, the hands should take the bat through the ball in the direction the ball is to travel.

In the mental picture of fighting for extension, the hands must be involved because they are the final summation of forces. At contact with the ball, the top hand should be facing the ball, not the sky. Although this will not always occur even on well-hit balls, trying to get to this hand position will help the hitter fight for extension.

Seeing the Ball

If the hitter abides by all the preceding rules but doesn't see the ball, all is for naught! To have a chance to hit well, the eyes must pick up the ball quickly, accurately, and clearly. Accomplishing this requires concentration and focus. Most pitchers have distinctive release points—above the ear, above the throwing-side shoulder, or below the throwing-side shoulder. The hitter should note the pitcher's release point.

Once he has a handle on the release point, he must go from *soft centering* to *fine centering*. Soft centering is a general focus in an area close to the release point, perhaps the letter on the pitcher's cap or his face in general. Fine centering is the hitter's best focus, yet this focus must be relaxed, not wide eyed. The hitter centers on the small window surrounding the release point, or if the pitcher gives him a clear view of the ball earlier, at that spot. It is widely accepted that the longer one fine-centers on a spot, the less clear it becomes. Thus the hitter does not want to fine-center until the moment he can pick up the ball. He should keep in mind that the earlier he can obtain information on spin, velocity, and location, the better his chance of being a successful hitter. He sees the ball, tracks it, and gathers all the information he can.

Putting the Ball in Play

A final comment concerning the physical approach to hitting is that the hitter should put the ball in play. He sees the ball hit the bat and puts the ball in play. In the stance, the chin starts above the front shoulder. By the end of the swing, the chin is over the back shoulder. The eyes stay on the ball. Hall of Famer Ted Williams once said, "If you choke up on the bat one inch, you will lose 5 percent of your power, but you will increase your efficiency 25 percent." The hitter does what it takes to put the ball in play.

VISUALIZATION AND MENTAL PREPARATION

It is one thing to know the mechanics of hitting; it is another thing to develop this desired skill in the swing. The following few pictures and thoughts may help hitters process the skill information into mental pictures that they can simulate in their swings.

Relax the Body, Focus the Mind. A hitter who grips the bat too tightly and has a rigid body that is tied in knots is often asked to relax. To react properly to a pitched ball, the hitter's body must be relaxed, but his focus, concentration, and visualization must be sharp. He must understand this point, because when a hitter tries to relax his body, he often relaxes his concentration as well, creating a sloppy swing.

Relaxed Upper Body, Strong Lower Body. As we narrow down this relaxation, we want the hitter's legs to be firmly planted on the ground, feeling solid and strong. The upper body should be more relaxed and ready to react. The hands will more than likely control the relaxation of the top half. If they are tight, the rest of the upper body will be also.

Quickness, Not Muscle. The hitter should remember this: "If you think strong, you think wrong." The normal reaction when a pitcher is throwing hard is to swing harder. This, in fact, slows bat speed and normally does not produce base hits. A hitter should concentrate on quickness to the ball. This will normally shorten the path to the ball and will produce a more productive at bat.

Tall, Loud Back Side—Short, Quiet Front Side. As the hitter pictures his swing, he imagines the back side driving the front side out of the way. He does not want the front side to pull the back side through, an action that produces a longer, slower swing. In other words, a loud back side produces energy and force, and the quiet front side produces less initial action. In reality, both sides work together. But the front side often opens up too early, the hitter loses plate coverage, and the front shoulder pulls the weight forward, causing a slow, sweeping swing.

The hitter also wants to produce a mental picture of a tall back side. A hitter will often drop his back shoulder below the level of his front shoulder or collapse his back knee, causing the back side to cave in. This causes the hitter to cast the bat away from the direction of the ball initially and will eventually produce a bat arc that is in an upward path. Obviously, this is a longer bat path and breaks the rule of rotating all body parts in the same path. This is normally referred to as *dipping*.

React, Don't Think. This is just another reminder to the hitter that he cannot do much thinking as the pitcher is preparing to throw the ball. He should trust his stuff and simply react to the pitch.

Evaluate Own Talent. Every hitter can control some areas of the strike zone better than he can others. Each hitter should know where his pitch area is in relation to the strike zone. Early in the count he should avoid swinging at strikes that are not in that area.

Evaluate the Pitcher. The hitter can observe the pitcher before his at bat or learn from each pitch that the pitcher throws to him. A pitcher often falls into patterns. What does he throw when ahead or behind in the count? Where does he throw most of his pitches? Does he work the fastball both in and out?

Some good questions the hitter can ask himself are "Can he strike me out?" and "Does he have a nasty strikeout pitch?" If the answer is yes, then his thoughts should turn to staying away from the strikeout counts. This may mean being less choosy early in the count. Remember, the object is to get the ball in play! If the hitter decides that the pitcher cannot, in his mind, strike him out, then he can be more patient early in the count.

Evaluate the Situation. Although we will talk about situational hitting in another chapter, it is worth noting that each at bat has different goals. When the infield is playing back with a man on third and less than two outs, the hitter's goals are different from those he would have when hitting with the bases empty. The batter must hit to the situation; he must know what he wants to do in each at bat.

Be Fearless.   To be a good hitter, the player must deal with the fear of being hit by the pitch. A person standing 60 feet, 6 inches away from him is about to throw a very hard object in his direction. It is natural to have fear, but the hitter must uncover and address this fear. The hitter must reach a point where he simply says, "I'd rather get hit by the ball than strike out or buckle my knees on a curveball that is approaching me."

Review the Strike Zone.   When the hitter starts to struggle, the strike zone usually appears bigger than it is. The outside corner looks to be almost unreachable. In like manner, the ball also appears smaller. The hitter would do well to revisualize the strike zone. An effective method is to tape the boundaries of the player's strike zone on a wall. Every umpire is different, but the strike zone for a six-foot hitter should be approximately 18 inches wide and three to four feet high, depending on his stance. The hitter stands in front of the wall and visualizes and practices his swing at each area of the strike zone.

Work the Count.   Simply put, the batter must make the pitcher throw strikes. A base on balls has a 100 percent on-base average! The hitter should not help the pitcher by swinging at balls out of the strike zone. The success ratio for a hitter over a full season often relates directly to the count when he hits the ball. Researchers, coaches, and players find this result every year when they look at batting outcomes in relationship to the count. When pitchers are ahead in the count (1-2, 0-2), the batting average will normally be 150 to 200 points lower than it is when the hitter is ahead in the count (3-1, 2-0). The critical counts, the 0-0 and 1-1 counts, swing the success-failure rate farther than any other count. In short, swinging at balls out of the strike zone can greatly increase the success ratio for the pitcher.

SKILL INSTRUCTION

The importance of isolating a particular phase of the total hitting skill becomes paramount to the hitter who strives for improvement. Concentrating on too many skills in a hitting-drill setting dilutes the mental attention needed for each individual skill. The objective in isolating each of the following skills is to have the hitter concentrate solely in one area until he establishes the skill as a natural reaction. A coach who tries to teach load, stride, and bat path at the same time will not get to first base!

Developing the Stance

Earlier in the chapter, we discussed the separate elements that make up a good stance (see pages 10-14). To evaluate your players, have them spread out in front of you in the outfield. All hitters should face you as though you are the pitcher (figure 1.5). As they take their stances, remind them of the elements of a good stance. You can use the checklist on page 12 to analyze each player's stance.

Figure 1.5 Analyzing the stance.

After you have evaluated each player's stance, have the players work in pairs. One player will observe his partner's stance and comment, and then they switch. People learn a subject better if they have to teach it. You should walk among the hitters to see that they execute the stance properly.

Encourage players to practice the stance in front of a full-length mirror.

Developing the Load

Earlier we discussed how a player should load before he strides (see page 14). You can use the setting you used to check the player's stance to check the player's load position. As the players face you in their stances, you go through a pitcher's windup. The only movement the players make is the load, which they should execute just before your release of the imaginary ball. Have the players freeze in the load position. Evaluate each player based on the checklist on page 16.

As with the stance, have players partner up and check each other. You may want to check each load as well.

Developing the Load and Stride

We are now going to travel from stance, to load, to stride. The load goes before the stride. To check that players are correctly moving from load to stride, you can use the setting you used to check each player's stance and load position. You go through the windup and deliver an imaginary ball. Remember, separation must occur between the load and the stride. The load starts just before the release of the ball; the stride starts at the release of the imaginary ball. Have each player freeze at completion of the stride. Have players partner up and grade each other, using the checklist on page 17.

Developing the Load, Stride, and Hip Rotation

Earlier we discussed hip rotation (page 18). Developing the skill to move from the load to the stride to correct rotation of the hips and torso requires patience and practice. To check how players move from load to stride to rotation, use the same setting you used to check stance and load position. This time, however, the hitter places the bat behind his back and holds it between his elbows across the lower half of his back (figure 1.6a). You deliver the imaginary ball, telling the hitter where the pitch will be located—in, middle, or out. The hitter separates the load, stride, and hip rotation, then freezes upon completion of the rotation (figure 1.6b). You can evaluate each hitter using the checklist on page 18.

Developing the Load, Stride, Hip Rotation, and Swing

Now it's time to develop the timing and mechanics of the total swing. Although only a slight separation in time occurs between each of these parts and the swing, they do need to follow in sequence—load, then stride, then rotation, then swing. To check how players move through the total swing, you can use the same setting you used to check stance and load position.

Hitters start with the proper stance. As you or a pitcher throws an imaginary ball, hitters follow the proper sequence. This is called *form swinging*. Players need

a

b

Figure 1.6 (a) The batter holds the bat behind his back and (b) rotates as if to hit the imaginary pitch.

to do this a lot and may find it helpful to practice in front of a full-length mirror. Hitters practice hitting all pitches in the strike zone, not just their favorite pitches. You call out pitch location.

Check load, stride, and rotation, but emphasize the points listed on the checklist.

Checklist for Developing the Load, Stride, Hip Rotation, and Swing

- The bat path is straight to the ball. The barrel finishes at the top of the front-side arm. Look for a short swing. Make sure that the front elbow does not go up to create a long path to the ball. The proper approach requires the hands to be higher than the front elbow with the barrel higher than the hands.
- The hips, shoulders, and bat travel in the same plane. Did the force of the swing stay on the same plane? Did the back shoulder remain higher than the front shoulder? Be sure the back knee did not collapse, causing an upward movement of the hips and bat arc.
- Check the power base. Did the weight transfer stay between the two feet? Is the stack aligned and in balance?
- At the point of contact with the imaginary ball, the hitter should try to feel the top hand spanking the ball and not hitting it with a palm-up judo chop. He drives through the ball. Remember, the bat does not travel in a perfect circle.

HITTING DRILLS

These drills can be done at home plate with the balls driven to fielders as well as in the situations described in each drill. You can use old tennis balls instead of baseballs. Young hitters, particularly, will have more success with tennis balls, and their confidence will increase as they see the ball explode off the bat. Late in a season, you may want to use tennis balls for older hitters to prevent tiring their hands.

Strike-Zone Swings

Purpose: To learn to hit in all areas of the strike zone.

Procedure:
1. From a plywood board or cardboard box, cut out the size of the strike zone and secure it to a fence or wall. (If neither is available, simply use tape on a wall.)
2. Draw nine balls in the rectangle of the strike zone—three across the top of the zone, three across the middle, and three across the bottom. Number the balls 1 through 9 (see figure 1.7).

3. The player stands in front of the strike zone and practices all parts of his swing on each ball in the zone.

Coaching Points: The hitter should remember the entire sequence—stance, load, stride, pivot, and swing. You can stand behind the hitter and call out the number of the ball at which the hitter should swing.

Dummy Swings

Purpose: To develop a proper swing while working with a stationary object.

Procedure:
1. You can use a boxing dummy, an old football dummy, tires secured to a pole or fence, or anything that is soft enough to give when the bat makes contact with it. The object can hang from a tree in the backyard! Sporting goods companies sell a dummy that is secured by a rope or chain at both the top and bottom.
2. The player practices all parts of his swing, making contact with the stationary object.

Coaching Points: This is a great way for the player to work on the total swing and develop hand speed and hand strength.

Batting Tee

Purpose: To develop the swing by hitting a stationary ball.

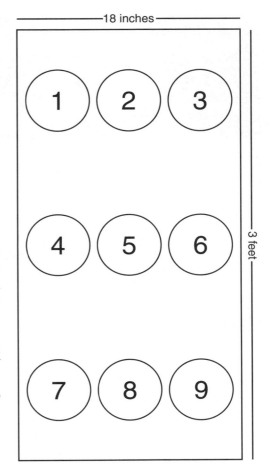

Figure 1.7 Strike zone.

Procedure:
1. This drill develops all facets of the swing. It requires a ball, a tee, and a hitter.
2. The hitter deliberately runs through all parts of his swing, making contact with the ball off the tee (see figure 1.8).
3. Most tees can be placed at different heights and in different areas of the strike zone. Hitting a ball off a tee can give a hitter a good feel for where to hit the ball in relation to the distance between the flight of the ball and the plate. To simulate an inside pitch, place the tee farther in front of the plate than you would to simulate a middle pitch. To simulate a middle pitch, place the tee farther in front of the plate than you would to simulate an outside pitch.

Variation: For the Double-Tee variation (figure 1.9), use two tees a foot apart or build a double tee that has the two tees a foot apart on a platform. The two tees should be at the same level and in a direct line to the pitcher. Place the ball on the tee closer to the pitcher. This drill is effective in working on the bat path to the ball. If the hitter hits the back tee before hitting the ball off the front tee, he is not moving straight to the ball.

Coaching Points: The batting tee may have been the earliest method that coaches and hitters used to isolate hitting phases. It still serves its purpose well for players of all ages and talents. With tee-ball leagues now popular for youth players, older play-

a   b

Figure 1.8 Batting-Tee drill.

Figure 1.9 Double-Tee variation.

ers may resent the practice of hitting a ball sitting on a tee. They shouldn't; major-league hitters use them all the time!

Soft Toss (Angle Toss)

Excluding live batting practice or machine batting practice, this may be the most widely used drill.

Purpose: To develop the proper swing.

Procedure:
1. The hitter faces a net or screen. The coach kneels approximately 10 to 15 feet away from the hitter at about a 45-degree angle to the hitter.
2. The coach tosses the ball underhand to the hitter to all areas of the strike zone (figure 1.10a).
3. The hitter tries to hit line drives (figure 1.10b).

Variations: Use a batting cage. The hitter sets up at the inside end of the cage. Challenge the hitter to drive the ball the length of the cage without hitting the top of the cage. This drill also can be set up in the backyard, using tied up or taped up rags that the hitter hits into a wall. Watch out for windows!

Coaching Points: This drill requires properly pitched balls but can be challenging. The hitter may want to isolate his swing and go without a stride. He uses everything else in his swing. What he will eventually realize is that the stride can cause more problems than it's worth. Sometimes in live batting practice or games it is natural and necessary to use a short stride, but it can also be a major problem for many

a

b

Figure 1.10   Soft-Toss drill.

hitters. The hitter in this drill often has more success without the stride than he does with it. Going without a stride can help identify a problem.

One-Knee Soft Toss

Purpose: To develop proper bat path to the ball.

Procedure:
1. Use the same setting as the regular Soft-Toss drill. Have the hitter kneel with his back knee on a throw-down base, pad, or towel on the ground. His front leg extends forward but is not fully straight. This position isolates the bat path.
2. The coach tosses the ball underhand to the hitter to all areas of the strike zone (figure 1.11a).

3. The hitter tries to hit line drives (figure 1.11b).

Coaching Points: The hitter may want to choke up some in this drill. A good progression is from One-Knee Soft Toss to standing Soft Toss with no stride, and then regular-stride Soft Toss.

a

b

Figure 1.11   One-Knee Soft-Toss drill.

One-Knee Soft Toss With Short Bat in One Hand

Purpose: To develop a feel of bat arc using only one hand.

Procedure:
1. Use the same setting as the regular One-Knee Soft-Toss drill.
2. Use a small bat or a sawed-off wood bat with a knob secured to the end (wrapping athletic tape around the end about 10 times will work).
3. The hitter holds the bat in his back hand and places his front hand in the armpit of his back arm.
4. The coach tosses the ball underhand to the hitter to all areas of the strike zone.

5. The hitter tries to hit line drives (figure 1.12).

Variation: Have the hitter hold the bat in his front hand (figure 1.13) and place his back hand in the armpit of his front arm. Hitting with the front hand is more difficult than hitting with the back hand, but it can enhance the feel of driving the knob to the ball.

Coaching Points: The hitter should work to develop the proper bat path.

Figure 1.12 One-Knee Soft Toss With Short Bat in One Hand drill.

Figure 1.13 Drill variation—the hitter holds the bat in his front hand.

Soft Toss With Two Balls

Purpose: To develop a short stroke.

Procedure:
1. Use the same setting as the regular Soft-Toss drill.
2. The coach places two balls in his hand with as much separation as possible.
3. He tosses both balls to the hitter and calls out "High" or "Low."
4. The hitter hits the higher or lower ball.

Coaching Points: This is a good drill to work on focus and short stroke. The coach may need a little practice time to acquire the toss skill.

Short Toss

Purpose: To develop a proper swing.

Procedure:
1. The coach sits in a chair directly behind an L-shaped pitching screen (figure 1.14a). A netting should be behind the coach to stop the flight of the ball. The best place to do this drill is at one end of a batting cage.

2. The hitter faces the coach approximately 20 feet away.
3. The coach throws overhand just above the lower part of the screen and close to the side of the upper half of the screen (figure 1.14b). He must be sure to stay behind the screen!
4. The hitter tries to hit line drives or ground balls.

Coaching Points: This drill, a favorite of many hitting instructors, simulates batting practice or live pitching without tiring pitching arms and requiring a full squad to shag balls. A coach who can throw well can work parts of the strike zone that the hitter needs to isolate. The hitter can perform the drill with or without the stride.

a

b

Figure 1.14 Short-Toss drill.

Pepper

This is another old but effective hitting drill, one we don't see enough anymore. Although it doesn't fully simulate the swing, a hitter will learn to control the bat.

Purpose: To learn to control the bat.

Procedure:

1. Four or five players position themselves in a straight line about 25 to 30 feet in front of the hitter.
2. One position player throws a ball to the hitter. The hitter hits it softly back on the ground. If the hitter can control the bat well, he can hit to the next guy in line (figure 1.15).
3. An error by a fielder moves him to the far left of the line.
4. After the hitter hits 10 ground balls, the player at the far right end of the line comes to hit. If the hitter misses a ball, he becomes the fielder at the left end of the line.

Coaching Points: Many variations of Pepper have been developed. The drill is a throwback to the old neighborhood games or stickball. Expect a few arguments!

Figure 1.15 Pepper drill.

Tracking the Ball

Purpose: To focus on the release of the ball and gain early information on where and when the ball will reach the plate.

Procedure:

1. The player steps into the bullpen to watch a pitcher throwing to a catcher.
2. He practices his load and swing while concentrating on the release point and the release and flight of the ball.
3. He visualizes his swing for each pitch, deciding exactly where he would hit it.

Variation: Another way to work on tracking is to have a pitcher throw balls marked with colored dots. Each ball has a dot of a different color. The hitter calls out the color as soon as he recognizes it. This drill creates competition and improves the hitter's ability to pick up the ball.

Coaching Points: This drill may be the best way to work on tracking the ball—picking it up clearly, quickly using fine tuning, and then watching its release and flight.

Stick Drill

Purpose: To develop a short stroke.

Procedure:
1. Get an old broom handle and cut off a three-foot piece of garden hose. Place the stick inside a portion of the garden hose.
2. The coach stands at approximately the same angle used for the Soft-Toss drill (page 30), but close enough to the hitter to be within range of the bat.
3. The coach points the stick toward an area of the strike zone. The hitter gets into his load position and tries to hit the tip of the hose.
4. The coach can move the tip when the hitter swings at the tip of the hose. The goal for the hitter is to hit the tip of the hose before the coach removes it. The coach can win the battle, but he should reward a short, quick stroke.

Coaching Points: A coach may want to use this drill only one time early in the season to drive home the point of taking a short stroke to the ball. The competitive hitter will shorten his swing to win the battle and will work for quickness rather than a muscular, hard swing.

Rapid-Swing Drill

Purpose: To develop a short stroke.

Procedure:
1. This drill uses the Soft-Toss setting (page 30); the hitter does not take a stride.
2. The coach rapidly throws five balls in succession to the hitter, throwing each ball immediately after the hitter hits the previous pitch.

Coaching Points: This drill forces the hitter to take a short stroke at the ball and keep a balanced power base.

Throwing the Bat Head

Purpose: To feel the forces going through the ball.

Procedure:
1. This drill should be done inside a batting cage for safety reasons.
2. The hitter swings at an imaginary ball and throws the bat head through the flight path of the ball.
3. On release, the bat should fly in a straight trajectory toward the area where the hitter wishes to hit the ball.

Coaching Points: This drill does not need to be used often. The hitter should feel all forces going through the imaginary ball. A hitter will often release the bat to his pull side although he was trying to hit the imaginary ball up the middle. This usually occurs because the hips rotate too far (spin hitter).

Balance Beam

Purpose: To develop balance throughout the swing. The drill offers an excellent way to check on whether the hitter maintains the proper stack throughout the swing.

Procedure:
1. Get a six-foot long two-by-six board. Approximately six inches in from each end, secure a two-foot long four-by-six board underneath the two-by-six. Place the two-by-six in the middle of the base boards at each end (figure 1.16).
2. The hitter stands on the two-by-six in a Soft-Toss setting (see page 31). The batter should wear tennis shoes in this drill.
3. This is a no-stride drill. The coach tosses balls that the hitter drives back up the middle.

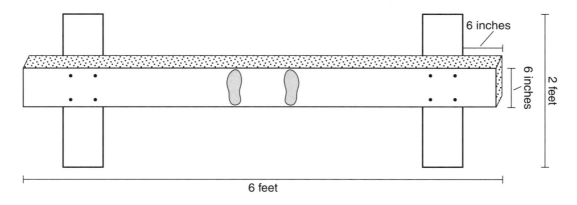

Figure 1.16 Setup for the Balance-Beam drill.

Coaching Points: The idea is to achieve balance throughout the swing. If the force of the swing is not going through the ball, the hitter will have to step off the two-by-six. A poor back-side pivot will normally cause the hitter to step forward off the two-by-six with his back foot. If the hitter leans forward at the waist toward the plate and loses the stack, he will slip forward off the two-by-six with his back foot. If he steps off the balance beam with his front foot in a backward step, he is probably spin hitting; his hips rotated too much. He may need to swing easy at first and then progress to a full swing. Balance is critical in a good swing.

Situational Hitting

The emphasis placed on situational hitting has diminished over the past 15 to 20 years. The advent of the high-powered aluminum bat, the introduction of the designated hitter, and the high salary premiums paid for home runs, RBIs, and slugging percentage have reduced the perceived value of situational hitting at most levels of play. For the baseball purist, situational hitting is one of the attractions of the game. If you watch closely, you'll see that the championship teams, in most cases, still use it to their advantage.

Anyone can win blowout ball games, but teams win championships because they win a large percentage of the close games. In many cases, they win because they can execute situational hitting. Teams usually advance to the playoffs because they have good pitchers who can beat good hitters. The playoff team that has hitters who can execute situational hitting is the team that often wins.

Situational hitting simply means that hitters hit to the situation presented by a particular at bat. With the bases empty and no outs, the at bat is different from the same situation with two outs. With a man on second and no outs, the at bat is different from the same situation with one out. In most cases, situational hitting does not require as much raw talent as does pure hitting. Consequently, players can learn it and use it to their advantage against dominating pitchers.

Situational hitting brings several other important advantages to the team:

1. It allows a less-skilled offensive player to contribute to the team's offensive success.

2. The player who gives his at bat to the team concept through situational hitting is identified as a team player.

3. Teams that work on situational hitting in practice will learn more quickly how to control the bat and the strike zone than those who do not work on this area of hitting.

The hitter must be able to adjust to numerous situations in a game. The following are some of the major situations to emphasize to your team. Bunting and fake bunting are forms of situational hitting because they move base runners. We will cover those situational hitting skills in chapter 3.

LEADOFF HITTER

The ultimate leadoff hitter always forces the pitcher to throw strikes and, in most cases, works the pitcher for five or six pitches in each at bat. Quite simply, he can take a strike and not panic. He knows he can put the ball in play. He often takes a strike on a 2-0 or 3-1 count unless it is his pitch in his zone. In some cases he takes it anyway.

Unfortunately, the leadoff hitter in your batting order sometimes leads off only in the first inning. Over a span of five or six games, everyone in your batting order will probably lead off some innings.

In situational hitting, the leadoff man forces the pitcher to throw strikes. If the hitter gets ahead in the count, he may be asked to take a strike. The surest way to reach first is by way of a base on balls. The probability of scoring increases dramatically when the leadoff hitter reaches first base. Thus coaches often tell their pitchers, "Get the leadoff man out, and your inning is halfway over!"

The hitter who comes to the plate with the bases empty and two outs is in a different situation. On the 0-0, 2-0, or 3-1 count, this hitter looks to drive the ball, hoping to get in scoring position. He knows that although a base on balls would put him on first, his teammates will probably need to put together a couple of two-out hits to score him.

The leadoff hitter must realize that he can help create a big inning by getting on base. Taking the 3-1 strike is frustrating to an individual hitter but not to a situational hitter. He knows that the pitcher has thrown four pitches and three of them were balls. The percentages say the pitcher will not throw two strikes in a row after missing on three of the four previous pitches.

MAN ON SECOND IN A NONFORCE SITUATION, NO OUTS

The two main situational hitting areas are at bats that occur with a runner at second and no outs and with a runner on third and less than two outs.

With a man on second base, no one on first base, and no outs, the hitter must step up for the team. His at bat must move the runner to third or possibly score him. The objective is to hit behind the runner. One school of thought says that the hitter must hit all balls to the right side. Another, and perhaps better, approach says that the hitter should hit the ball to the right of where the runner on second leads off. This larger target gives the hitter a chance to control a wider area of the strike zone with authority and perhaps drive the runner home. One drawback of hitting to that area is that the ball hit back to the pitcher will not move the runner. The base runner's rule is always to advance to third on a ball hit at him or to his back side, except if the ball is hit to the pitcher. Still, hitting to a wider zone that extends to the left of second base will not only move more runners but also drive in more runs.

In this situation, the right-handed hitter must lay off the strike thrown on the inner third of the plate early in the count. He should look for a pitch on the outer two-thirds of the plate. The hitter must be sure to hold his power base (weight within both feet) and let the ball get a little deeper (closer to the plate as opposed to out in front of the plate). He wants to be sure to lead with the knob of the bat to ensure that he stays on the inside of the ball. The hitter should not completely give away his at bat. He must aggressively drive the pitch. Obviously, the surest way to get the runner to third is by a sacrifice bunt, but particularly early in a game, the team should go for more than one run. The hitter must just stay off the inside pitch that requires pulling the ball.

A left-handed hitter should stay off the pitch on the outer third of the plate early in the count. He is looking for a pitch that he can drive to the middle or right side of the field. His job is easier than the job of the right-handed hitter.

Work with your team on this area of situational hitting. With less than two outs, a runner can score from third in many more ways than he can from second. Develop this skill in batting practice and through the Short-Toss drill (page 34).

MAN ON THIRD, LESS THAN TWO OUTS

This circumstance requires a different kind of at bat. Remember, RBIs are always better than hits! The hitter should get the runner in for the score.

The hitter should note the position of the infielders. Are they back, halfway, or in? Regardless of where they are, the hitter's point of emphasis should be to stay above the ball in the approach and not overswing. He doesn't want to pop up or strike out.

With the infield back, a simple ground ball will almost always score the runner unless it goes back to the pitcher. Many coaches emphasize hitting to the middle of the field because the middle infielders are too far away from the plate to throw out the runner at home; a ground ball hit hard to a corner infielder may result in the runner being thrown out trying to score. Although hitting up the middle may be a legitimate approach, it can be too restrictive for some hitters. Emphasizing line drives and ground balls with good bat control is a good rule. The more experienced hitter sometimes likes to drive the ball in the air for a sacrifice fly or even more. But this attempt often produces pop-ups or short fly balls. Unless the hitter is highly skilled, I don't recommend this tactic.

With the infield playing in or halfway, the hitter should approach the situation the same way. The probability of driving a ball through the infield increases when the infielders play closer to the plate. Coaches don't like to play in because doing so can give the opponent a chance for a big inning.

This situation does not require a great offensive player. He must simply stay on top of the ball, control his swing, and put the ball in play. Every coach becomes annoyed when the hitter takes a called third strike in this situation, so the hitter should give in and put the ball in play! The chances for good things to happen are great, even on poorly hit balls.

You can present this skill in the Short-Toss drill or Soft-Toss drill, but players learn best in live batting practice.

HIT-AND-RUN

A well-executed hit-and-run appeals to the baseball purist. The hit-and-run is usually used in two situations. The traditional one is with a man on first or men on first and third. The other hit-and-run situation is with men on first and second.

Man on First or Men on First and Third

To execute the hit-and-run, signal the man on first to attempt to steal second. Either the second baseman or the shortstop will break to the bag to receive the throw from the catcher. The hitter swings and tries to hit the ball to the unoccupied area (either second base or shortstop). Normally, the second baseman covers second base with a right-handed hitter and the shortstop covers with a left-handed hitter. For our purposes, we will assume that the defense follows this rule.

The hitter has a clearly defined situational-hitting task. He has three areas to address:

1. He should swing at the pitch unless it is in the dirt or so far out of range that he cannot make any contact. In either of these situations, the pitch is so poor that the catcher will be unlikely to catch the ball cleanly and throw out the runner stealing from first. But if the catcher has a chance to make a clean catch and throw, the batter must swing at the pitch. Even if he misses the ball, the catcher will have a somewhat tougher time throwing out the runner at second.

2. The hitter should hit the ball on the ground. If he cannot hit the pitch to the proper area of the infield, he should at least hit it on the ground. The runner will make it to second and will be in scoring position. A fly ball can create double plays and will usually result in an out without advancing the runner.

3. The hitter should hit the ball to the designated area. The hitter must not only swing at the ball and hit it on the ground but also hit it to the unoccupied area of the infield.

To execute the hit-and-run properly, the hitter must not overswing. The priority must be a solid, controlled swing. His power base (weight within both feet) must remain solidly intact. He must make extra effort to stay on top of the ball, approaching the ball with the barrel above the hands and keeping the hands higher than the front elbow. He leads the swing with the knob of the bat toward the ball and lets the ball get depth (closer to the plate). He attempts to stay inside the ball on the swing. The idea is to hit the top half and slightly inside the ball. He must not overswing and must stay back.

The Pepper drills that we talked about in chapter 1 are also a good way to learn to control the bat (see page 35). The Short-Toss drill is another drill that works the hit-and-run swing (page 34). Of course, the best way to practice the hit-and-run is off live batting-practice pitching.

Men on First and Second

A similar execution is desired with runners at first and second although it is less important to hit the ground ball to a particular area of the infield. Remember, the third baseman will move to cover third, opening another hole in the infield. The job of the hitter is to put the ball on the ground.

TWO-STRIKE SWINGS

The two-strike swing is a different situation for the hitter. He needs to make adjustments with the priority of getting the ball in play. Highly skilled hitters will not need to alter their swing much, but most hitters will need to change their attitude and physical approach from what they use with a 2-0 or 3-1 count. The hitter must give in. We referred to this quote by Ted Williams earlier, but it's worth mentioning again: "If you choke up on the bat one inch, you will lose 5 percent of your power, but you will increase your efficiency 25 percent."

Choking up on the bat or getting off the knob gives a hitter better bat control. The hitter might also concentrate on keeping his power base intact and staying inside the ball. Remember, most strikeouts occur on the outer half of the plate. The batter should shorten the stroke and put the ball in play. Some hitters like to move up in the batter's box or move closer to the plate. The hitter must find what works best for him and then practice it before he faces a two-strike count in a game! Hitters rarely practice their two-strike swings enough. Short toss, soft toss, and batting-practice settings are areas to work on two-strike swings.

Bunting

With the advent of the aluminum bat and big-inning baseball, the bunt is used less often than it was in the past. Even so, the bunt can be an effective weapon in close ballgames, and it still plays an important role in championship baseball. Let's talk about the various forms of bunting.

SACRIFICE BUNT

In most cases a team executes the sacrifice bunt when they consider the runner on base a potential critical score. Teams do not sacrifice much early in the game because most coaches play for the big inning. At any rate the bunter must realize that the sacrifice bunt is not the time to relax just because he is not swinging. He must bear down!

When sacrifice bunting a runner from first to second, the bunter should normally try to bunt to the first-base side. When sacrificing a runner from second to third, the bunter should bunt to the third-base side. He should make every effort not to show the bunt early unless he incorporates the fake bunt–slash off the sacrifice bunt. Once the first and third basemen know the bunt is on, they can quickly close ground and possibly get the lead runner. As the pitcher commits to throwing to home plate, the hitter should square around. Remember, the pitcher can still try a pickoff or quick step-off move to see if the hitter shows the bunt too early. With a runner on second, the pitcher can do an inside move to second by bringing his front knee up and then circling it toward second in a continuous move. The bunter must be sure that the pitcher commits to throwing to home plate.

Square Around

The bunter can square around in several ways to put himself in a fundamentally correct bunting style. The three movements we will cover are the heel-toe pivot, feet square around, and feet partially square around.

Heel-Toe Pivot. Without moving his feet from their original spot, the hitter simply pivots on his back foot by placing his weight on the ball of his foot and rotating his heel away from the pitcher (figure 3.1). He will place weight on the heel of his front foot and move his toes toward the pitcher. This technique may be difficult for some younger players because it requires a balanced move. The advantage of this method is that the hitter doesn't have to move much and he can more easily execute a fake bunt–slash.

Feet Square Around. While staying in the batter's box, the hitter moves his back foot forward until it is even with his front foot (figure 3.2). The feet should point toward the middle of the field, placed a little wider than shoulder-width apart. This is perhaps the best method to teach to young players.

Feet Partially Square Around. Although similar to the feet square around method, in the feet partially square around method the bunter does not bring the back foot completely forward. The toes point more toward second base for the right-handed hitter (figure 3.3) and toward the shortstop for the left-handed hitter. This is the most common way of executing the sacrifice bunt.

Figure 3.1 Heel-toe pivot.

Figure 3.2 Feet square around.

Figure 3.3 Feet partially square around.

Stance

If the bunter executes the square around properly, the shoulders and hips should be square to the pitcher, that is, they face the pitcher. The knees are slightly bent. The top hand slides almost halfway up the bat and assumes a pinching grip that covers the backside of the bat. The bunter holds the bat parallel to the ground at the top of the strike zone and extends it forward. The hitter's elbows should be down, and he should be able to see the back of his bottom hand. Seventy percent of the bunter's weight should be on his front foot. His eyes should see directly over the bat. The bat should cover the entire plate; if the bunter were to drop the bat after getting in his stance, the end of the bat would extend to the outer corner of the plate.

Execution

The objective is to aim the bunt toward either third base or first base, soft enough that it causes the corner infielder to come at least halfway between the plate and his base to get the ball, and hard enough that the catcher can't field it. Obviously, the bunter should not hit the ball upward because a diving corner infielder, pitcher, or catcher may catch it in the air. This possibility puts the base runner in a tough spot because he doesn't know if the ball will be caught.

The right-handed hitter bunting toward first base should move the knob of the bat forward so that the bat is almost parallel to the third-base line. When bunting toward third, he points the bat toward first base, placing the bat nearly parallel to the first-base line. The left-handed bunter simply reverses the preceding information.

The following are some basic rules for executing the sacrifice bunt:

1. The hitter should bunt the top half of the ball. The bat should move in a slightly downward motion on contact.

2. A good mental picture that the bunter can use is to catch the ball on the bat, which is what really happens.

3. The bat should be held loosely to produce a softly bunted ball. To deaden the ball further, an advanced bunter can bunt the ball closer to the end of the bat.

4. The bunter should not jab at the ball. If he has properly squared his body and the bat has complete plate coverage, he should not have to jab at the ball. Last-minute jabs, usually caused by poor original plate coverage, often result in poor bunts.

5. The most critical area in the execution of the bunt is to bend the knees and keep the eyes just over the bat. The body must move down on low pitches. Do not stay straight up and drop the arms. Keep the eyes just over the bat, and bend the knees!

6. Finally, the bunter must not be in a hurry to run to first. He must bunt the ball before starting to first.

FAKE BUNT–SLASH

The objective with the fake bunt–slash is to show the bunt early enough to draw the corner infielders in and possibly cause the second baseman to start toward first to cover the bag. The bunter should not square around too early, however, or the defenders may smell a rat!

The following are some basic rules for the execution of the fake bunt–slash:

1. The hitter fakes a commitment to the bunt just before the pitcher's movement from the stretch. If the pitcher has a pattern of holding in the set position, the hitter has a better chance of faking the bunt. If not, the hitter must use his instincts.

2. The heel-toe pivot is the best method of squaring around. Moving the feet around in the box usually results in poor execution. The hitter fakes the bunt using the upper body, with little movement of the lower body. Seventy percent of the weight remains on the back foot.

3. The top hand slides upward on the bat, leaving only an 8- to 10-inch gap between the hands as the bat moves forward into a presumed bunting position.

4. Just before the pitcher's release, the hitter brings the bat to the top of the strike zone. He brings the lower hand up the bat to just underneath the top

hand. He stands in a normal hitting stance except that he is choking up on the bat. A critical mistake hitters often make is to bring the bat back in a low arcing movement without getting it back to its proper position. The bat should come straight back to its proper position.

5. The hitter does not overswing but concentrates on hitting the ball on the ground. If the fake works, he has created many holes in the infield.

6. Unless a hit-and-run is part of the plan, the hitter should make the pitcher throw a strike. His chances of successful execution decrease if the ball is not a strike. Some hitters, such as the drag bunter, often do not want to give up the element of surprise, and they try to hit regardless of whether the pitch is a ball or strike. Remember, the best way a hitter can move runners is with a base on balls or by working the count in his favor.

PUSH BUNT

The batter uses a push bunt either to reach first on a base hit or to move runners over.

Right-Handed Hitter

The right-handed hitter tries to push the bunt past the pitcher toward the second baseman. This bunt is especially effective against a left-handed pitcher who falls off the mound toward third base.

When the pitcher prepares to release the ball, the hitter simply moves his top hand up the bat approximately six to eight inches. The lower hand keeps the knob close to the chest. The batter should hold the bat firmly as he pushes it toward the ball, aiming his movement toward the second baseman. The hitter should try to bunt the inside portion of the ball. At contact, the hitter's right foot should move forward toward the ball.

Left-Handed Hitter

Not to be confused with the drag bunt down the third-base line, the push bunt normally is used against a right-handed pitcher who falls to the first-base side. The idea is to push the ball toward the shortstop. The left-handed batter does not use this bunt as often as the right-handed batter does the push bunt to second.

The left-handed bunter simply reverses the execution of the right-handed push bunt. He should emphasize keeping the right foot in place before contact. The initial step should be with the left foot toward the pitcher. To get a jump out of the box, the left-handed bunter often lets his right foot step toward first base, but doing this will prevent him from making proper directional contact with the ball.

DRAG BUNT

The drag bunt is used primarily to obtain base hits. Even if not successful, the drag bunt will normally move the corner infielders in and give the hitter a better chance to drive the ball past them, either in that at bat or in a later one. The bunter should make directional mistakes in foul territory, not to the area in front of the pitcher.

Good drag bunters try to make contact with the ball toward the end of the bat. Contact at that location cushions the ball and keeps it from rolling as far. Holding the bat less firmly in the hands can also promote a soft touch. Obviously, the longer the batter can wait before showing his intention to drag bunt, the greater the element of surprise.

The batter should observe three key rules in drag bunting:

1. He should bunt only at strikes. A critical mistake is bunting at a bad pitch only because he has the element of surprise.

2. Proper ball placement is more important than the jump out of the box. Drag bunters often start moving toward first before laying down the bunt.

3. The batter must not give up. Drag bunters have a tendency to become discouraged with unsuccessful drags more quickly than they do with hitting the ball into outs. The player must give it a chance. If he has an aptitude to drag bunt, his on-base average will probably be between 30 and 40 percent. He can't give up after three unsuccessful tries! The worst he has done is to improve his percentage on the next attempt and bring the corner infielders in, which will increase his hitting percentage.

Right-Handed Hitter

Like the push bunt, the drag bunt is executed primarily from the hitting stance. Most right-handed hitters are comfortable dropping the right foot slightly back as they bring the knob of the bat approximately six inches in front of the left hip (figure 3.4). The right hand slides up the bat approximately six to eight inches as the

Figure 3.4 A right-handed hitter executing the drag bunt.

barrel comes forward and down. The knees bend, and normally there is a bend at the waist. To drag the ball toward third, the bunter points the end of the bat toward first. To drag the ball toward first base, he points the knob toward third.

Left-Handed Hitter

The left-hander simply reverses the execution of the right-handed drag bunt. He must be sure not to start his movement to first base before contact. Some left-handed drag bunters prefer to slightly step toward the pitcher with the left foot as they make contact with the ball (figure 3.5).

Figure 3.5 A left-handed hitter executing the drag bunt.

SUICIDE SQUEEZE OR SAFETY SQUEEZE

A chapter on bunting would not be complete without discussion of the suicide squeeze and the safety squeeze. Championship teams can execute these offensive maneuvers when the runner at third is deemed a critical score.

The suicide squeeze is an all-or-none play. The runner at third takes his normal lead. If the pitcher is working from the windup, the runner gets a good walking lead. If the pitcher is working from the stretch, the runner takes a longer stationary lead, but he will not be able to gain as much ground as he could with a walking lead. The runner and the batter must wait until the pitcher reaches the point of no return. (This point normally occurs when the pitcher's pitching hand goes back and just before his front foot touches the ground.) At this point, the runner at third breaks for home plate, and the batter squares around to bunt the ball regardless of whether it is a strike or not. If the bunter misses the ball, the runner is, in baseball terms, dead meat. The priority for the batter is to get the bunt down. The direction of the bunt is not as critical as making contact with the ball and putting it on the ground. The batter should try to avoid bunting the ball back to the pitcher.

The safety squeeze is not an all-or-none play, but it requires a little more finesse by both the batter and the runner at third. The runner at third does not break for home until he sees that the batter has put the bunt down and it is not going back to the pitcher. The batter bunts only at strikes and must bunt the ball clearly away from the pitcher.

The mechanics for both of these bunts are similar to those of the sacrifice bunt, although the heal-toe pivot is not advised. The bunter brings the back foot forward, gains good balance, and puts the bunt down away from the pitcher. Obviously, a premature show of intention gives the corner infielders a chance to close in on the play and decrease the chance for a successful squeeze. The bunter should wait until the pitcher's hand starts taking the ball back toward second.

BUNTING DRILLS

As with almost all skill work in baseball, the best time to work on skills is during live games, intrasquad games, and batting practice. Because of time constraints, however, each player often gets only a few repetitions. Drill areas outside a game setting produce sound opportunities to learn skills.

The team should practice all phases of bunting in each batting-practice segment. It is well worth noting that bunting attempts in games do not follow a patterned sequence. Many swings occur between bunt attempts. As a basketball free thrower could tell you, it is far better to stop the scrimmage game for 45 seconds, shoot free throws, and resume the scrimmage than it is to shoot 50 free throws at the end of practice. The same is true in bunting. To provide gamelike preparation, have your players alternate bunting and taking full swings rather than executing five bunts in a row.

You can design a scrimmage in several ways to integrate opportunities to work on specific areas of the game. You may want to put the bunt sign on periodically or simply play a bunting scrimmage so that the team can work on bunt defense as well. Devise what you like, but this is the ultimate way to drill before a game.

The following drills can help teach bunting skills.

Group Form Bunting

Purpose: To execute correct timing and mechanics in bunting form.

Procedure:
1. Players spread out facing the coach as though he were the pitcher (figure 3.6a).
2. Working from the stretch position, the coach executes the pitching motion and throws an imaginary ball.
3. The batters square around as the coach moves his throwing arm toward second. They place themselves in bunting position and freeze (figure 3.6b).
4. The coaches evaluate their timing and mechanics.

a

b

Figure 3.6 Group Form Bunting drill.

5. After the coaches evaluate the players a few times, the players partner up and coach each other.

6. The coach can call out the location of the pitch (i.e., high and outside, middle low, etc.). He also can call out which base the bunters should bunt to and check bat angle.

Coaching Points: This drill technique is good for drilling all forms of bunts and fake bunts. Refer back to proper execution of each of these skills. By freezing the execution, the coach can give hitters a checklist for examining their freeze positions themselves.

Three-Man Drag-Push-Sacrifice Drill

Purpose: To execute proper mechanics and bunt the ball.

Procedure:

1. Players form groups of three throughout the field. One player is the designated bunter. The other two stand 25 to 45 feet away from the bunter (distance depends on age and skill). The two fielders spread apart, taking the positions of the pitcher and first or third baseman.

2. The pitcher throws the pitch to the bunter, who bunts to the baseman (figure 3.7a).

3. The baseman fields the bunt and then becomes the new pitcher. The batter squares to the new pitcher (figure 3.7b).

a

b

Figure 3.7 Three-Man Drag-Push-Sacrifice drill.

4. The pitcher throws to the bunter, who bunts the ball to the original pitcher (who is now in the position of the third baseman).

Coaching Points: Drag and push bunts can also be used in this drill. Alternate bunts and then rotate the players so that each player has an opportunity to bunt. Players should not pitch the ball hard because accuracy is the key.

Fungo Bat–Golf Ball Bunting Drill

The thinner fungo bat and smaller ball force better focus and precise execution and should have a good carryover to the actual bat and ball.

Purpose: To emphasize focus and execution.

Procedure:
1. Because practice and skill are required to pitch a golf ball with accuracy, the same person should be the pitcher throughout the drill. The bunter stands at home plate. The pitcher stands 20 to 45 feet away.
2. The pitcher throws the golf ball to the bunter, working for accuracy, not speed.
3. The bunter executes the bunt using the fungo bat.

Batting-Machine Contest

Player focus is heightened if competition is involved. The batting machine is a good tool to use because it is usually more accurate and consistent than someone throwing the ball and does not tire as quickly. Fewer arguments result as well!

Purpose: To execute the bunt with a little more pressure on results.

Procedure:
1. Mark off the drill area with a chalker, cones, bats, or helmets. Whatever is available will do, but make the boundaries clear (see figure 3.8).
2. Players take turns executing bunts from balls pitched by the batting machine.
3. To win points, bunted balls must stay in the boundary areas. Balls that do not go past the halfway point between home plate and the base are normally considered good, but the ball must roll out of the catcher's reach.

Coaching Points: The boundaries depend on the size of the field and the age of the

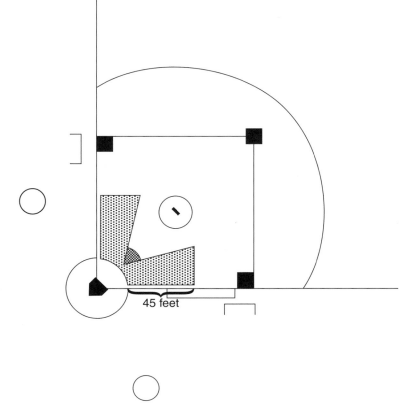

Figure 3.8 Boundaries for Batting-Machine Contest.

players. Place the boundary far enough from the pitcher's left or right so that he could not get the leading runner. The base lines are the outer boundaries. Keep totals and post results. Players who are competitive will enjoy the drill and improve their bunting.

Fake Bunt–Slash Drills

Purpose: To learn to execute proper mechanics.

Procedure:
1. Do this drill in the Soft-Toss setting (page 31).
2. When the pitcher gives the command, the bunter starts the drill. As the bunter completes his fake-bunt movement, the pitcher underhands the ball to the hitting area.
3. The batter must get his bat back properly to hit the ball.

Variation: Try this drill off a batting machine. As the person feeding the batting machine brings the ball up to place in the machine, the batter initiates the fake bunt. As the feeder places the ball in the machine, the hitter returns to his hitting stance and hits.

Coaching Points: You should also incorporate this drill into batting practice and scrimmages as the next progression. In batting practice the pitcher should throw from the stretch.

4

Baserunning and Stealing

Courtesy of Texas A & M University

"He was out by an inch!" "The throw beat him by a half second!" Inches and seconds—games are won or lost by a few inches or a fraction of a second. Certainly infielders, outfielders, and catchers all work on the premise that they must do all they can to gain the advantage of time and distance. They spend hours, days, and months working on defensive mechanics to improve on inches and seconds. Similarly, every base runner should realize that he too can work to place the inches and seconds in his favor. A brief hesitation, a turn too wide, an arcing path— these and many other practices can cause a team to lose by an inch or a second.

CRACK OF THE BAT

Baserunning starts with the crack of the bat. The ball goes into play, and nine defenders go into motion to stop the base runner. The clock starts and the race is on!

Ideally, the hitter has hit the ball with his body still properly stacked with his weight on the balls of his feet. A left-handed hitter who loses his stack and reaches across the plate to hit an outside pitch, or a right-handed hitter who leaves his weight on his heels or on a caved-in back leg, will not get a good start out of the box. Proper hitting technique gives a hitter a good chance to be quick on his start to first base.

The right-handed hitter should start his run by stepping first with his right foot toward first base (figure 4.1). The left-handed hitter should open his right foot and cross over with his left foot toward first (figure 4.2). The first four or five steps are critical in gaining maximum speed.

Figure 4.1 The right-handed hitter starting to run.

Figure 4.2 The left-handed hitter starting to run.

To go forward, the body must lean forward. The lean starts from the legs, not simply by bending at the waist. The player should angle his entire body forward.

Short, choppy steps are critical. The length of the stride increases as the runner approaches maximum speed, but he must take short steps to reach maximum speed quickly.

To take short strides with good explosion, the arms must move in the same rhythm as the legs. Leg movement and arm movement complement one another. Short, quick steps require short, quick arm movements.

The elbows should remain close to the body, bent at a 90-degree angle. When the elbows get away from the body, the hands usually cross the midline of the body, causing the body force to go sideways instead of forward. If the arms are more straight than bent, the runner will not have quick, short arm movements and his strides will be too long.

The quickest path between two points is a straight line. Any deviation from that line increases the distance and time required to reach the base—by a half second or by an inch, which may be the difference between being safe or out! The easiest way for a player to run in a straight line is to be looking at the point he wants to reach. Watching a fielder make a play or putting the head down to run hard is not a good technique.

Infield Ground Ball

On an infield ground ball, the batter–base runner cannot assume that the fielder will make the play at first. He should play the game to its fullest, running all out because anything can happen. The batter–base runner should keep these points in mind:

1. He should run *through* first base, not *to* first base. He must be going full speed as he crosses the base. A good rule is to go full speed one step past the bag.

2. The runner should step on the front part of the bag. If inches are critical— and they are—he should touch the nearest part of the bag.

3. He should not leap at the bag. The final step to the bag should be short, not long. A long, leaping step costs precious time.

4. A slide is useful only in avoiding a tag. A feetfirst slide takes extra time, and a headfirst slide can cause injury.

5. The player should always run full speed to pressure the fielders. As routine as the play may appear and as upset as the batter may be that he did not hit the ball well, he should play the game hard. Anything can happen!

Ball Hit to the Outfield

The batter–base runner must presume that any ball hit to the outfield will be extra bases until the defense proves otherwise. He should always run full speed to first and take an aggressive turn, never assuming that the outfielders will make the play. When he gets a chance to be a base runner, which may happen only once or twice a game, he must go full out.

FIRST BASE

The runner's strategy as he approaches first base depends on the situation—the number of outs, the inning, the score. An aggressive approach to first base is the first step to scoring. In this section we will cover taking the turn at first, taking a lead and a secondary lead at first, and advancing to second.

Taking the Turn at First

It would be easy to get a chalker and draw the path a person should take in getting a proper turn at first or any base (figure 4.3). But every runner has different abilities. Some can take shorter turns than others. Each player should practice his turn with a stopwatch if possible.

The objective here is twofold. First, the runner completes most of the turn before he reaches the bag. Doing this will put him at a more familiar distance to the next bag. From that point he can make a better decision about whether to advance. Second, ultimately he wants to make the turn close to full speed without taking an excessively wide angle before reaching the bag. The player must practice to find the best angle for him. Going in a straight path to within 10 feet of first base may cause him to slow too much to turn properly, but starting the turn 70 feet away from first adds too much distance and takes too much time. It is easier to go full speed in a wide arc, but doing so increases the distance and takes more time. The player should find what works best for him.

As the runner approaches the bag, the angled turn requires a leaning in to prevent the centrifugal force of the turn from shifting body weight to the right side. An outward shift would result in a wider turn as the runner attempts to control his balance. The runner should dip the left shoulder toward the mound and let the right elbow move away from his body.

The runner should step on the inside of the bag. Because the base is anchored to the ground, the runner can push forcefully off it to finish his turn and begin his movement to the next base. The fastest way to round the bag is to touch it with the left foot. Developing the timing to do this requires practice. The runner should not shorten the final steps to the bag just to get the left foot on it because taking the extra step consumes too much time.

The batter–base runner should be aggressive on the turn. If the ball is in left field, he may complete the turn farther away from first. When he hits the ball to center field or

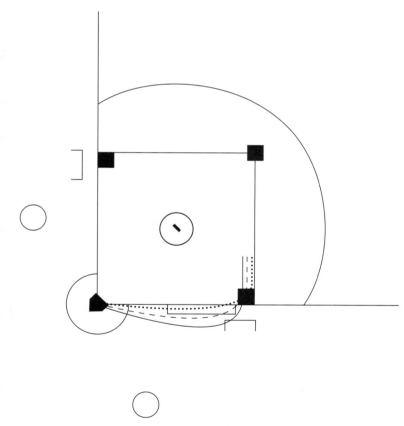

Figure 4.3 Different players will take different turns at first.

right field, the turn cannot be as long because the outfielder could throw behind him for a back-door play.

The runner should keep in mind that the more outs there are in the inning, the more daring he can be. He can take a greater chance in advancing to second base with two outs then he would with no outs.

When a batter gets a hit with a runner on second who is attempting to score, the batter–base runner should advance to second when his instincts tell him that a play will occur at home. He can also advance to second if he makes a good turn and sees that the outfielder has thrown the ball to home plate too high to be cut off by the cutoff player.

Taking the Lead at First

Before taking the lead, the runner should quickly review the situation. He should know how many outs there are and remember the rule in baserunning at first base: do not make the first or third out at third base. He gets the signs from the third-base coach while on the bag. He never leaves the bag until he knows where the ball is and is prepared to give the player with the ball his full attention.

The base runner should take his full lead before the pitcher begins his windup into his set position. Most successful pickoffs occur while the pitcher is going up or coming down into his set position and the base runner is in the process of getting his lead. The runner should take his lead as the pitcher gets the signs from the catcher.

The movement off the bag should be in a straight path toward second base. The initial move off the bag should be one normal shuffle step followed by a crossover step with the left foot going behind the right foot. Using these steps will give the runner immediate quick distance into the initial stages of the lead. The crossover must be done with the left foot behind the right foot. If the left foot goes in front of the right foot, movement back to first base on a pickoff move is hampered.

The length of the runner's lead depends on his ability to get back to the bag without being picked off. The distance varies among players. Normally, a good lead is the distance a player can cover with a crossover right step in front of the left foot and a full dive back. The lead should be 12 to 15 feet for a mature player (figure 4.4).

Once the player attains his initial lead, he uses smaller shuffle steps—a deliberate shuffle of the right and left feet toward second base. The feet should never come close together and should never be more than an inch or two off the ground. The knees should be bent, and the body should be in a position to react to a pickoff attempt.

Upon completion of the lead, the right foot should be slightly open and slightly (four to six inches) behind a straight line between first base, the left foot, and second base. This positioning will help the runner make a good jump on a steal attempt. The body should be in its best reacting position with the weight on the balls of the feet.

Secondary Lead

The secondary lead occurs after the pitcher has committed his pitching motion to home plate. The idea is simply to gain as much ground as possible and yet be able

Figure 4.4 The lead at first.

to return to first base safely should the catcher decide to attempt a pickoff with the first baseman.

The secondary lead should stay in a straight path to second base and is normally done with aggressive shuffle steps facing home plate (figure 4.5). A good base runner will develop proper timing so that he is moving toward second when the ball is hit. Obviously, he will reach second more quickly if he is already in motion rather than stationary. He achieves this by not taking a secondary lead so long that he must stop as the ball enters the strike zone because he fears being picked off by the catcher. The base runner shuffles with his body facing home plate. Timed properly, the final left-right steps have his right foot open and his body slightly turned toward second as the ball reaches the strike zone.

If the base runner has taken an aggressive secondary lead and the ball is not hit, he is vulnerable to being picked off by the catcher. The proper technique is to jam the right foot, cross over, and aggressively move back to first. The base runner must not be lazy and wait to see if a pickoff attempt is coming. He should always assume that the catcher will make an attempt.

Advancing to Second

When advancing to second on a ground ball, the base runner should run in a straight path until he knows that the ball has gone through the infield and a force-out play will not occur at second. Turning before knowing there will be no play at second will cost inches and possibly the play.

When advancing to second on a fly ball, the runner must determine whether the fielder will be able to make the catch and whether he will be able to advance by tagging up.

When at first, the runner does not tag up unless he is sure that the outfielder can catch the ball or unless the ball is clearly in foul territory. Another rule the base runner can use at all bags is simply not to tag up if he cannot advance on the caught ball. A short fly ball to the left fielder that appears as if it will be an easy catch is an example. If the fielder catches it, the runner cannot advance, but if the

a   b

Figure 4.5   Aggressive shuffle steps help the runner take his secondary lead.

fielder drops it, the runner wants to be far enough off the bag to get to second before the fielder's throw there for a force-out.

When tagging up, the runner faces the bag he wishes to advance to and places the foot closer to the play on the bag. If the runner is at first and the ball is hit to right field, he puts the right foot on the bag. On a foul pop-up to the catcher, the runner places the left foot on the bag. This positioning gives the runner open vision to the play without affecting body balance. The foot not on the bag should be a short step away from the tagging foot in a straight path to the next base. The runner starts tall. As the fielder makes the catch, the runner bends his knees and explodes off the bag.

The runner should tag up on all foul balls. Fielders often must make running catches with movement away from the field and perhaps close to fences. Anything can happen, so the runner should tag up.

On deep fly balls, the base runner's instincts must tell him with some degree of certainty whether the catch will be made. When in doubt, the runner should not tag, but if he feels the catch will be made and that he can advance by tagging up, he should do so.

The situation changes with a man on second or third or both. On a normal fly ball when the second-base runner, or third-base runner, or both are tagging with a chance to advance, the runner on first should also tag. Instincts are important here. If the runner on first feels that the outfielder has a legitimate play on the man advancing from the tag at either second or third base, he should tag and advance to second. In his initial step to second, he needs to know that the base runner at

Figure 4.6 Prior to touching second base, the baserunner looks to the third base coach for assistance on a ball hit to right field.

second or third is indeed going to try to advance, and he needs to make sure the outfielder is attempting to throw that runner out. Again, instincts are critical in this situation.

SECOND BASE

Every base runner's first goal should be to reach scoring position as a step toward the ultimate goal of scoring. Moving into second puts him in position to score on a solid hit or move into third. Whether he takes an aggressive turn around second to move into third immediately or stops at second and waits for the next opportunity to move to third depends again on the situation.

Taking the Turn at Second

The runner follows the same rules in taking the turn at second as he does at first. If the ball is between the left-field line and the right fielder, the base runner must decide whether to advance to third. The time to gamble is with one out—a runner should never make the first or third out at third base. If the ball is hit behind him (from the right fielder to the right-field line), the runner should look at the third-base coach for assistance because turning back to see the ball would cause him to slow down (figure 4.6). The runner should pick up the third-base coach well before touching second. When the third-base coach signals him to stop, the runner should touch the bag and immediately find the ball. The outfielder may have dropped it or misplayed it after the third-base coach made his decision.

When using the third-base coach while advancing to second or third base, the runner should assume that the coach will advance him. By going hard until the coach stops him, the runner will be sure not to slow prematurely.

Advancing to Third

Before taking his lead, the runner should review the various situations that could come up:

1. On a tag play, he must not take the risk of making the third out at third base.

2. Likewise, the runner should avoid making the first out at home plate.

3. If the runner on third is tagging on a normal fly ball and the runner's instincts tell him that a play will occur at home, he should tag and advance if he sees the runner at third go to home plate and the throw from the outfield is to home. When in doubt, the runner should not advance.

4. On a deep fly to the outfield that may or may not be caught, the runner should tag if there are no outs. With one out, the rule is to get off the bag and hope the ball falls in. If it does, the runner can then score. If the runner starts off the bag but than realizes the play will be made, he should go back and try to tag.

5. At second base with less than two outs, the runner should always check the placement of the outfielders. Are they in, back, moved to the pull side? Knowing the outfielders' positioning will help the runner get a better jump on line drives or short fly balls.

6. In a nonforce situation, the rule for the runner at second is to advance to third on a ground ball hit at him or behind him (to the right side). The two exceptions are to hold at second on a ball hit back to the pitcher and to advance on a slow ground ball that brings the third baseman in on the grass.

Lead at Second With Less Than Two Outs

As with the lead at first, the base runner establishes the lead before the pitcher's movement to the stretch position. With less than two outs, the lead should be in a direct path between second and third base (figure 4.7). The lead should be at least a step longer than the lead at first base. The rule at second is that the lead should be two steps and a dive away from the base. A long lead is necessary only when a steal attempt is on, when the runner is trying to distract a nervous pitcher, or when the third-base coach wants to force a middle infielder to move closer to the bag to hold the runner. The runner must avoid going back toward second when the pitcher commits to home plate. This wrong-way movement frequently happens when a runner takes too long a lead and a middle infielder fakes a pickoff attempt.

Figure 4.7 Lead at second with less than two outs.

Lead at Second With Two Outs

In a published study conducted in 1971, I found that Division I baseball players as well as college males who did not play baseball established a faster time to home plate by leading off second base at a point wider (toward left field) than the point directly in the base path (Mark Johnson, "Two Outs and a Man on Second," *Athletic Journal* 53 [January 1973]: 46, 75). Although the wide lead (figure 4.8) moves the runner farther from third base and is thus not used with less than two outs, it allows the runner to score more often on close plays at home plate. For the mature player, the lead should be approximately 10 feet off second base in a straight line to third base and then at a 90-degree angle 17 feet from that point toward left field. The runner must be sure to avoid being picked off at second base when using this lead. It is neither a long lead nor a stealing lead.

a

b

Figure 4.8 The wide lead off second.

Secondary Lead at Second

The secondary lead, the additional lead the runner can achieve when the pitcher starts his delivery to home plate, can obviously be a little longer at second because the catcher has a longer pickoff attempt to second than he does to first or third. As he does at first, the runner should time the lead so that the final left-right steps are in progress as the ball arrives in the strike zone. Some players are more comfortable taking their secondary leads at second and third base with their bodies facing the next base or home plate. Others prefer the shuffle lead that concludes with the left-right steps facing the next base or home plate. With the two-out wide lead, the runner should be sure that his secondary lead moves in a straight path toward an area two steps behind third base toward left field. The runner should not reduce the turn angle created by the wider lead by moving toward the base path in his secondary lead.

THIRD BASE

Third base is the final stop before scoring a run. This is not the place to relax. The runner should concentrate and plan to score.

Taking the Turn at Third

The runner must remember not to start his turn until he knows there is no play at third. When taking the turn at third base (figure 4.9), he uses the same turn he did at first and second. The key in this turn is to watch the third-base coach, not the ball. The runner always goes full speed as though the coach is planning to send him to home plate. The coach is the runner's eyes.

Advancing to Home

The runner is now 90 feet from scoring. He should be alert and plan ahead. Before taking his lead, the runner mentally reviews the several situations that could come up—the passed ball or wild pitch and, with less than two outs, the fly ball, the line drive, or the ground ball.

Passed Ball or Wild Pitch. The runner's willingness to gamble increases with the number of outs. With no outs he must be sure he can advance.

Fly Ball With Less Than Two Outs. The runner always tags on fly balls to the outfield. If the ball is uncatchable, the runner will score anyway. On short fly balls or Texas Leaguers, the runner will have to go by his instincts. In most cases it is best not to tag, although the diving catch will occasionally cost the runner a chance to score. The runner always tags on fly balls or pop-ups in foul territory.

Line Drive With Less Than Two Outs. As he should on all line drives, the runner freezes until he sees the ball fall in. This practice is critical at third base because the runner can normally score easily if the line drive does fall.

Ground Ball With Less Than Two Outs. Perhaps the most critical decision the runner will need to make is whether he can score on a ground ball, but he can make 95 percent of the decision before the ball is hit. Normally, if the infield is playing

a   b

c   d

Figure 4.9 The runner goes full speed around third, looking to the third-base coach for instructions.

back, the runner at third advances on a ground ball unless it is hit back to the pitcher. If the corners are in, the runner advances only on a ball hit to the middle infielders. If the entire infield is in, the runner at third base will normally see the ball through the infield before advancing. Some exceptions are the high-bounding ball or slow roller that would allow the runner at third to score even if he were not planning to advance. Again, instincts are important here.

Some speedy, aggressive teams make an effort to get a good, clean jump at third when they initially surmise that the ball is going in a downward angle off the bat. It doesn't matter to them whether the infielders are in or not. A good jump usually allows the player to score if the fielder must move to either side to get to the ball. Obviously, a runner using this strategy can be caught if the ball is hit back to the pitcher.

Lead at Third

As mentioned earlier, some players are comfortable directly facing the advancing point when moving from second toward third or from third toward home plate. Others prefer to shuffle step. Whichever method he uses, the runner must be sure that his final left-right step faces home plate. The lead at third should always be in foul territory (figure 4.10). The runner does not want to be hit by a screamer off the bat while in fair territory because he would be out.

Pickoff attempts by the pitcher are rare at third base because the third baseman is not holding the runner on and pitchers and coaches fear a bad throw that would result in a score.

Pitcher in Windup Position. When the pitcher winds up, the runner normally takes a shorter lead and faces home plate. As the pitcher starts his windup, the runner uses a bent-knee walking lead, finishing with a left-right step as the ball enters the strike zone. This is not a long lead. The farther a runner gets off third, the more likely he is to stop before the ball is hit because of the fear of being picked off by the catcher. He will reach home plate faster by using a shorter lead with movement going to home plate than he would by using a long lead with no movement as the ball reaches the strike zone. If the catcher catches the pitch, the runner jams and returns to third on the inside of the base (figure 4.11). By returning to the base in the throwing lane, the runner makes the catcher's pickoff throw more difficult. The runner should remember that catchers pick at third much more often with a left-handed hitter at the plate.

After the runner has jammed and starts his initial retreat to third, he should make sure the catcher's throw back to the pitcher is accurate. A poor throw could mean an easy score.

Pitcher in Stretch Position. The runner takes a slightly longer lead when the pitcher is in the stretch position, similar to the lead he uses at first base—one step and a dive back to the bag. The runner faces the infield in a shuffle-lead motion.

Figure 4.10 The runner stays in foul territory when taking a lead at third.

Figure 4.11 The runner jams and returns to third if the catcher catches the pitch.

a
b

Secondary Lead at Third

As the pitcher commits to home plate, the runner may again shuffle step or turn and use a bent-knee walking lead. Whichever he prefers, he must finish with a left-right step facing home plate as the ball reaches the strike zone. Again, he stays in foul territory.

BASERUNNING DRILLS

As with all phases of the game, players must practice baserunning. The best way to practice these skills is on the base paths with a stopwatch. All athletes enjoy competition. Improving on their previous times or competing with their teammates will produce exciting, productive skill drills.

Without question the best way to work on baserunning skills is with live pitching and hitting situations, either in intrasquad games or batting practice. In both cases, runners can be placed on bases, creating hitting and baserunning situations.

Base-on-Balls, Hit-by-Pitch, and Home-Run Drill

Purpose: To warm up before baserunning practice.

Procedure:
1. Players line up at home plate.
2. Each player steps into the batter's box and responds to the coach's command to simulate one of the following situations:
   - Base on balls. Players should run at a minimum of 75 percent of their maximum speed after a base on balls. This is a good spot to drill this into a habit. Nothing bad ever comes from hustle.
   - Hit by pitch. This drill can help teach proper response to being hit by a pitch. Encourage players not to flinch or buckle and hold up the game. Encourage them to respond with toughness by immediately hustling to first base. The player should not look at the pitcher or make any movement toward him.
   - Home run. Encourage players to hustle in making their home-run trots. They should not jump, express jubilation, talk, or show up the pitcher by making a slow trot or by standing at home plate and watching the ball go over the fence.

Coaching Points: Use a rapid-fire approach with this drill. No more than 10 yards should separate the players.

Infield Ground-Ball Drill

Purpose: To encourage hustle and reinforce proper running technique.

Procedure:
1. Players line up at home plate.
2. A player steps into the batter's box, assumes his batting stance, and either takes a full swing at an imaginary ball or hits a ball thrown by a pitcher.

3. If you are using a live pitcher, time the batter's speed to first base with a stopwatch. The clock starts when the batter hits the ball and stops when his foot touches first base.

Coaching Points: Remind players that even on a play that appears easy, they should go hard to put pressure on the defense.

Outfield-Hit Drill

Purpose: To encourage hustle and reinforce proper technique for taking the turn at first.

Procedure:
1. Like the previous drill, this drill uses live pitching or an imaginary swing.
2. Place a cone, glove, or other object on the outside corner of the first-base bag to remind runners to use the inside corner of the bag when turning (figure 4.12a).
3. Place a cone or coach approximately 10 feet away from first base toward second base, angled about 10 feet off the base path toward right field. This target will encourage runners to begin the turn before reaching first base and will help them get a good push off the bag and in line with second (figure 4.12b). If the runner does not turn in front of the cone or coach, he is taking too wide a turn.
4. Use a stopwatch. For more mature players, the difference between the run through the bag and the turn should be no more than three- to four-tenths of a second.

a   b

Figure 4.12 Outfield-Hit drill.

Coaching Points: Remind players that a hit to the outfield is a double until the fielder proves otherwise. The runner takes an aggressive turn. If you are using an imaginary ball, call out where the ball was hit. The runner will advance relatively far toward second if the ball reaches left field, a moderate distance if the ball reaches center field, and a short distance if the ball is hit to right field.

Turn-at-Second Drill

Purpose: To drill proper technique for taking the turn at second and watching the third-base coach.

Procedure:
1. This drill uses a secondary lead at first base. The turn at second can be done using the same setup that was practiced at first base.
2. The coach calls out where the ball is hit. On a hit to right field, the runner practices using the third-base coach (figure 4.13).

a

b

Figure 4.13 Turn-at-Second drill.

Coaching Points: Be sure that the runner checks the third-base coach at least 25 feet before touching second base.

Man on Second in a Nonforce Situation With Less Than Two Outs

Purpose: To practice moving to third or home.

Procedure:

1. You can run this drill with four players in a group leading off second base or with one player. Have a full defensive infield with a pitcher on the mound.

2. The player or players attain their secondary leads as the pitcher simulates a throw to home plate. A fungo hitter hits balls to various parts of the infield (figure 4.14).

3. The runners must decide whether or not to advance.

Figure 4.14 Man on Second in a Nonforce Situation With Less Than Two Outs drill.

Coaching Points:
Remind players to advance only on balls hit at them or behind them, with the exceptions that they don't advance on a ball hit back to the pitcher and they do advance on a ball that brings the third baseman in.

Tag-Up Drill

Purpose: To reinforce proper tagging technique and situational running.

Procedure:

1. You can work on tag ups at all bases and set up the situation of your choice. In particular, all teams should practice tag-up situations at second base (figure 4.15).

2. With no outs, runners tag on all deep balls that may or may not be caught; with one out, runners do not tag.

3. The outfield should be set up defensively, and a fungo hitter should hit deep fly balls to the outfield. The coach will call out how many outs there are.

Coaching Points: Check to make sure that the runner is tagging the base with the foot closer to where the ball is going (figure 4.15a). Check also to be sure that he starts tall and then bends his knees to begin his push off the bag (figure 4.15b).

Figure 4.15 Runner tagging at second.

a   b

Dive-to-the-Bag Drill

Purpose: To practice retreating to the bag when a pickoff is attempted.

Procedure:

1. This drill is best practiced on a foul line in the outfield.

2. Using the foul line as first base or second base, several players take their leads at the same time.

3. A pitcher or coach stands in front of the group and, from the stretch position, simulates either a pitch to home plate or a pickoff attempt.

4. Each runner practices the step and dive back to first base or the two steps and dive back to second base.

Coaching Points: By using the grass area rather than the dirt part of the infield, the drill is less punishing and allows for numerous practice attempts.

BASE STEALING

An important aspect of offensive baseball is the ability to steal bases. Having a base-stealing threat on the bases can play havoc with the pitcher, catcher, and middle infielders. The pitcher may lose concentration on the hitter and may throw more fastballs. A base stealer can force a middle infielder to play out of position simply to hold him close to second base. And, of course, the successful steal moves the base runner into scoring position.

Good base stealers are not always the fastest runners on the team. They usually have adequate speed and are sometimes the fastest players on the team, but the secret of their success is that they use proper steal technique and watch the pitcher for clues that will give them a good head start.

The critical element in stealing a base is getting a good start—a good jump, in baseball lingo. Bases are stolen in the first four or five steps, so this is the area that needs to be addressed.

Obviously, the lead is also critical. Coming up a few inches short on a steal attempt could be the result of being a few inches too short on the lead. On the other hand, a long lead leaves the runner vulnerable to being picked off and often results in a poor jump. Each runner must find the longest lead that will allow him to get back to first base on a pickoff attempt as well as get a good jump on a steal attempt.

Straight Steal of Second

The right foot should be slightly opened and placed slightly behind an imaginary straight line between first base, the left foot, and second base. The runner must be in his best reacting position. His knees should be bent, his elbows should be bent with the hands in front of the body, and his body weight should be on the balls of his feet (figure 4.16).

The initial step of the jump is made with a crossover step by pushing off with the left foot and stepping across and in front of the right foot. This should be a rather short step made in a direct path toward second. The runner must be sure not to step first with the right foot because doing so will slow the start. Because the right foot is slightly back and slightly opened, there is no need to move the right foot first.

The upper body is also important in the initial explosion toward second. The elbows should be bent at about a 90-degree angle with the hands in front of the body. As the runner starts the jump, the left leg crosses over toward second and the back of the right hand thrusts toward second base. These two motions bring force toward the target and help turn the upper body in the right direction (figure 4.17). Keeping his head in alignment with his body, the stealer should glance in as the ball reaches the plate to make sure he knows if and where the ball is hit. Taking a quick glance without raising the head should not impede his run.

Figure 4.16 The runner's knees and elbows are bent in front of his body.

Figure 4.17 The runner's body turns toward second.

Note that the runner directs the initial force toward second, not upward. A young player will often explode upward, leaving his body too tall and straight. Subsequently, he will need to readjust his body alignment. The runner usually takes four short steps before he reaches full stride. To start his run, he uses short, choppy steps with short, quick arm pumps. The arms and legs work together.

Delayed Steal of Second

The delayed steal does not require exceptional speed. A runner normally attempts it with a left-handed hitter at the plate because the hitter momentarily obstructs the catcher's view of the runner at first. The delayed steal can also be effective if the catcher has the habit of going to his knees after catching the pitch or if the middle infielders do not break toward second after each pitch.

The base runner executes the delayed steal by extending the secondary lead by a shuffle or two. The rule is to take three full shuffle steps. As the final left-right shuffle hits the ground, the runner opens the right foot and breaks for second base. He should have an easier time reaching full speed because of the momentum of the extended secondary lead. If the timing is correct, the runner should start his sprint to second just as the catcher catches the pitch. If the runner takes the extended lead properly, the first baseman will be unable to identify the steal attempt and will not be able to alert the catcher. If the catcher stoops or goes to his knees, or if the middle infielders are not moving toward second, the base runner will have an excellent chance of stealing successfully.

Steal of Third

Although the throw from the catcher to third base is almost 40 feet shorter than the throw to second base, many base runners find stealing third to be easier than stealing second. Four main reasons support this thought:

1. The runner at second can take a much longer lead because no defender is standing on second base.
2. The lead allows the runner to gain movement and momentum before making his break to third.
3. The pitcher must turn 180 degrees toward second rather than 90 degrees toward first. The turn requires more time, allowing the runner to gamble a little more on the lead.
4. The pitcher cannot see the runner's movement when looking toward home plate. With a runner at first, the pitcher can see movement peripherally even when not looking at first.

The main reason coaches do not use the steal of third base is simply because the runner is already in scoring position and they don't want to gamble on losing the runner with an attempted steal. In contrast, the steal of second is attractive because unless you move the runner into scoring position, two hits will likely be required to score the run.

The two primary preconditions to stealing third base are taking an extended lead and having movement going toward third when the pitcher commits to home plate. Although many coaches order their players to steal second by flashing a sign, most instruct their players to steal third only if they have achieved the extended lead and are moving toward third when the pitcher commits to home plate. An exception would be if men were on first and second and the steal was called on a 3-2 count.

The extended lead lengthens the established lead of approximately two steps and a dive back to second base. The runner achieves the extended lead by taking short shuffle steps or quick bouncing steps. These steps or bounces should be short and close to the ground because the runner is vulnerable to the pickoff. A good runner will play with the pitcher, extending the lead and retreating with identical shuffle steps or bouncing steps.

If the runner achieves an extended lead, then proper timing becomes the key ingredient to the success of the steal. The runner usually attains proper timing by taking a few short shuffle steps or bounces just as the pitcher looks back at home plate in preparation to pitch. If the pitcher pauses or looks to second base again, the runner must retreat. This pattern can continue over multiple looks from the pitcher or multiple pitches. Timing is critical. Good timing will give the runner a good jump and will establish the momentum that will allow him to reach full speed more quickly than if he had started from a stationary position.

Ideally, the initial step toward the committed steal should be a crossover with the left foot. But because the pitcher's movement dictates timing, the runner may become caught in his shuffle steps with more weight on the left foot when he commits to third. If this occurs, he should use a short open step with his right foot.

BASE-STEALING DRILLS

Leads and Steals From First

Purpose: To reinforce proper lead and steal technique from first base.

Procedure:

1. Place three throw-down bags down the right-field line behind first base approximately five feet apart. Four players can then work at one time (figure 4.18a).

2. Place a pitcher on the mound. Call out to the runner or send signs from the third-base coach's box about what play you want to see. Steals, the hit-and-run, and delayed steals all can be practiced in this drill (figure 4.18b). Players can work on their leads in all cases.

3. If no sign is given, players work on their secondary leads as the pitcher throws to home plate.

4. Competition can develop about who reaches second base first or who gets to a line 15 feet away from his lead first. You can also use a stopwatch.

a

b

Figure 4.18 Leads and Steals From First drill.

Coaching Points:
Make sure that runners cross over on their initial jumps and do not take a short open-up step with their right feet when you call for the steal. Check that players use proper leadoff movement, take good secondary leads, and when you give no sign, they jam back to the bag.

Leads and Steals From Second

Purpose: To practice proper technique for getting a lead at second and stealing third base.

Procedure:
1. Using a similar setup to what you used at first, have four players lead off second base and a pitcher on the mound.
2. Call to the players which lead you want them to work on—the lead with less than two outs, the secondary lead, and the lead to take for an attempted steal of third.

Coaching Points:
Players must take their two-out leads one at a time. Runners don't use the two-out lead in steal attempts.

Leads From Third

Purpose: To practice scoring from third base on hit balls, passed balls, and wild pitches.

Procedure:
1. Four players may go at once. Place a pitcher on the mound.
2. A fungo hitter simulates hitting fly balls, line drives, or ground balls as the pitcher simulates the throw to home plate.
3. Have the pitcher throw balls in the dirt to the catcher so that the runners can work on attempted scores on passed balls and wild pitches. You call the number of outs.

Coaching Points: Runners tag on fly balls and freeze on line drives. For passed balls and wild pitches, runners read the play and react accordingly.

Sliding

W e've all seen it many times. The preschooler comes out onto the field after the bigger guys have finished their game. He begins to run, usually starting at home plate, maybe clockwise or perhaps counterclockwise. He strains for the next bag and slides to it in a cloud of dust. He is safe! The slide works! He gets up and dusts himself off, his face aglow.

Many baseball players learned to slide in just this way. Did he make his first slide on his left or right side? Whichever way he slid, there is a good chance that he will slide on that side for the rest of his baseball-playing career.

Without question, the best-kept secret in baseball is the instruction and execution of the proper slide. Why? No one was taught. They just started sliding, some correctly and many incorrectly. This phantom method has been passed down from generation to generation—you just slide.

Several characteristics are part of being a good base runner, but on top of the list would probably be aggressiveness. A good correlation exists between aggressive base runners and good sliders. Likewise, the poor base runner is often poor at sliding. Either consciously or unconsciously, he avoids taking the risk at the next base because sliding hurts. Sliding poorly is not like swinging and missing or throwing a pitch that misses the strike zone. Improper slides hurt. Players break wrists, hands, and fingers, jam their knees, and acquire huge abrasions called strawberries.

Coaches avoid teaching sliding because they lack knowledge and because injuries could occur. Although sliding is a natural movement for some players, as hitting is for others, most players must be taught how to slide. Players can learn how to use the slide to reach the next base without experiencing the pain and injuries that result from poor technique.

STRATEGY OF SLIDING

In amateur baseball, players slide for two basic reasons—to reach a base going full speed without going by it and to avoid a tag. In professional baseball, players also use slides to break up a double play. In all cases, once a player makes a decision to slide, he must never change his mind. Indecision causes more injuries than any other part of sliding. If a runner has a doubt about whether he should slide, he always slides.

The proper sliding technique is an aggressive movement. While being aggressive, however, the base runner must also be relaxed. A rigid, nonrhythmical sliding movement increases the risk of injury. Aggressiveness and relaxation are a result of confidence, of the player's knowing that he has the proper technique because he has learned and practiced it.

Sliding must be explained and mentally pictured as nothing more than a gradual lowering, or controlled falling, of the body. It is not a leap or jump or dive. It is more of a glide on top of the ground.

Finally, injuries often occur in sliding because the player places too much of his weight on one area of the body during the slide. Good sliding technique disperses the friction over a large area of the body, thus decreasing abrasions and jolting.

TEACHING AREA AND DRESS

Certainly, various methods can be used to teach sliding. Most agree that players learning to slide should wear pants of heavy material and long-sleeved shirts. They should be in stocking feet. The heavy material and long sleeves help avoid abrasions, and the stocking feet cannot catch in the ground as cleats can (figure 5.1).

The areas used to teach sliding are more varied. Sliding pits with saw-dust or other loose material are often used, but they tend to cause a leaping or jumping approach. Watered-down areas in the grass outfield or blankets on gym floors are other options. One of the best surfaces for learning the feetfirst slide is a piece of long cardboard, obtained from new refrigerator boxes or mattress boxes. When opened, the boxes present a long surface to slide on. Place a loose base toward the end of the cardboard. The advantages are numerous:

1. The player can slide easily.
2. Full speed is not necessary when first learning to slide.
3. The player is relatively safe from jarring.
4. Sliding on cardboard is fun.
5. The cardboard can be used on any surface.

Figure 5.1 When learning to slide, players should wear long-sleeved shirts, pants of heavy material, and no cleats.

One hazard is that floor-burn abrasions occur with direct skin con-tact with the cardboard. Players learn immediately that they must fol-low proper technique to prevent this from happening.

The following sections describe the most common of the many slide variations. When players receive proper instruction and practice suffi-ciently, sliding will be more fun, cause fewer injuries, and produce a more aggressive offensive attack.

BENT-LEG SLIDE

The bent-leg or straight-in slide (figure 5.2) is the most popular slide in baseball. Most other slides, with the exception of the headfirst slide, are adaptations of this basic slide. The bent-leg slide is one of two slides that get the slider to the bag at the earliest possible moment (the headfirst slide is the other).

The following coaching points are useful in teaching the bent-leg slide using card-board and the suitable dress mentioned earlier.

Have players sit on the ground with their legs spread, their hands on the ground at their sides, and their upper-body weight resting on the palms of their hands and buttocks. Players bend one leg under. Either leg is fine. Players will find that one leg is more comfortable in the bent position than the other is.

The shape of the legs should resemble a figure 4 with the lower portion of the bent leg crossing just under the knee of the straight leg. The bent leg should remain parallel to the ground. If it does not, too much friction will be placed on either the knee or the ankle during the slide, resulting in abrasions.

The cleats of the bent-leg foot should face away from the ground to prevent the cleats from catching in the sliding surface. If players are in stocking feet while learn-

a   b

Figure 5.2   The bent-leg slide.

ing to slide, check to make sure that the soles of their feet are facing away from the ground. Emphasize the importance of not catching the cleats in the ground.

The straight leg stretches forward with the knee slightly bent so that it won't be jammed when it meets the bag. The foot should be approximately 6 to 10 inches off the ground to avoid catching the cleats.

The buttocks should remain completely on the ground. Sliding on one side or the other results in the painful strawberry. The upper body leans back until both shoulder blades almost touch the ground. The neck is bent with the chin down so that the player can see the bag and the area in front of him.

The arms are bent at the elbows with the hands up. Holding grass or dirt in the hands will help prevent the normal reaction of trying to break the fall with the hands. Hand and wrist injuries often occur because players let them hit the ground with the slide.

As the players sit on the ground after moving through these steps, place a mental picture of the glide in their minds.

- The glide is a controlled fall with the final push-off made by the bent leg.
- The first contact with the ground occurs on the outside lower half and knee of the bent leg, then on both sides of the buttocks, then on the lower back.
- The relaxed, extended leg is lowered, and the heel of the foot makes contact with the front edge of the base.

The texture of the surface and the speed of the runner will determine when he starts the slide. Mature players sliding on a normal infield texture will start to slide approximately 10 to 12 feet from the bag.

Upon completion of these dry runs while sitting on the ground, players slide on the cardboard. They begin to run approximately 15 yards from the cardboard and slide at three-quarter speed until they establish a good feel for the slide. The coach should place himself on both knees at the side of the cardboard near the end and hold the loose base. You may need a player on each side of the cardboard to keep the cardboard from shifting, depending on the surface under the cardboard.

POP-UP SLIDE OFF THE BENT-LEG SLIDE

The pop-up slide is similar to the bent-leg slide except that the runner finishes by standing on the base, ready to advance if possible. Base runners use it in various situations—when a tag will not be made in time, when a bad throw could be approaching, or when a player wants to get to the bag quickly without slowing down.

The player uses the fundamentals (figure 5.3) of the bent-leg slide with a few exceptions. The runner should start to slide a little closer to the bag (approximately 8 feet rather than 10 feet). His upper body remains in a sit-up position with the body weight extending from the bent lower leg to the buttocks. The body's center of gravity should remain between the knee and buttocks and not extend past the waist. The extended leg is slightly bent and raised three to four inches. The slider contacts the bag with the instep of the extended leg.

As the player makes contact, the leg straightens and thrusts the upper body forward. If the slide is aggressive, this should be enough to carry the body to an upward position. If a runner has problems achieving this position, he can use his hands to thrust himself upward, although he should rarely need to do this.

a

b

Figure 5.3 The pop-up slide off the bent-leg slide.

HOOK SLIDE

The hook slide (figure 5.4), also known by many coaches as the 93-foot slide, is used to avoid a tag. The decision to use the hook slide is usually based on the premise that the ball will beat the runner to the sliding area but will be slightly off target. The hook slide is not the fastest slide because the back leg rather than the front leg tags the base. Hence, we hear reference to the 93-foot slide.

Use the following coaching points to teach the hook slide. Players should slide approximately 2 to 4 feet to the side of the base, starting approximately 8 to 10 feet from the base. When sliding to the right side, the runner pushes off his left foot before starting his slide. Neither leg should be in a tucked position. The outside of the right leg (calf and thigh) should make contact with the ground first. The leg should be bent slightly with the bottom of the foot pointed in to prevent the player from catching the cleats.

The left leg should be relatively straight with a slight bend in the knee. The inner part of the left leg should contact the ground with the bottom of the foot pointed out and the toe pointed forward in anticipation of contacting the bag with the shoestring. The player must not bend the left knee any more than necessary to hook the base. The more he bends the knee, the longer it will take to make contact with the base. The player should distribute more weight to the right part of the buttocks.

Figure 5.4 The hook slide.

a

b

The upper body should almost be in a flat position with the head up and the eyes on the bag. Although it is difficult to do, the player should try to keep the hands and elbows from jarring the ground.

In the final mental picture of the hook slide, the legs should be in a scissor position with body weight on the right side. For a hook slide to the left side, simply reverse the procedures for the right side.

HEADFIRST SLIDE

Little has been written concerning the headfirst slide (figure 5.5). Its increased use in modern baseball may be due to the aggressive playing style of Pete Rose. Or perhaps players use it more today because of the widespread belief that it is the quickest approach to the bag. Whatever the reason, the headfirst slide is becoming a bigger part of today's game.

Although few studies have been made, experience and observation would lead one to believe that an aggressive headfirst slide will get the runner to the base more quickly than other slides because the runner does not have to move his center of gravity back (as he does in the leg-first approach). Instead, he moves it forward in the direction he is going.

The headfirst slide is not advantageous in the following situations:

1. Tag plays at home if the catcher can block the plate
2. Force plays
3. Breaking up a double play

Once a runner commits to this slide, he must continue through at full speed. The headfirst slide does not allow the runner the same opportunity to advance as the bent-leg slide does because he cannot pop up as easily from this slide.

The following coaching points can help you teach the headfirst slide. Use a soft grass area in the outfield. You may want to water the area before conducting the drill. If you have a spare tarp, water on top of it will be sufficient. Players should wear long-sleeved shirts and long pants.

a

b

Figure 5.5 The headfirst slide.

Begin by giving your players the proper mental picture of the slide. It is simply a glide on top of the grass, not a dive or a leap.

The runner begins by lowering his upper body and placing his center of gravity farther in front of his legs. As his body lowers and his weight shifts forward, he makes his final thrust forward with only one leg. On the final thrust forward, the body must be low to the ground as if the player were running and then gliding on top of the water. The arms stretch forward with only a slight bend in the elbows. The player keeps his head up so that he can see the base. His chest, legs, and arms should all be in one plane, parallel to the ground. The forearms, chest, and thighs make simultaneous contact with the ground. The hands catch the base to avoid jamming the fingers.

Problem areas to watch for are players using their elbows or hands to break the fall, players not keeping their chests up, and players using their knees to break the fall. Remind players to keep their bodies straight but not rigid.

To practice the technique, use dives back to first base on pick-off attempts. You can also use short runs with good aggressive explosion on the final thrust. Once the players can feel the slide, they will become faster, more aggressive, and better able to perform it.

PART II

Defense

Properly played defense can completely control the flow of the game of baseball. Every coach wants to develop a team that plays consistently, does not beat itself, meets every situation with poise, and is able to make the great play. A strong defensive player can make his mark on a team, find his way into a contributing position, and earn a chance to play while continuing to improve and develop as an offensive player. Outstanding offensive players excite many baseball fans, but no one ever forgets the catches of Willie Mays and Ken Griffey Jr., the throws of Roberto Clemente, the defensive plays of Brooks Robinson, Roberto Alomar, John Olerud, or the sparkling plays of many current major-league shortstops. They make the plays that stay with you, the plays that you see young players trying to copy.

Great defense can turn the momentum of a game and break the spirit of your opponent. Poor defense can dishearten a team, make it appear poorly coached, and prolong the game.

All successful defensive players are alert and have great anticipation skills. They visualize the upcoming play and seem to will the ball in their direction. Through anticipation, study of the game, and knowledge of their opponents' offensive skills and their pitchers' strengths and weaknesses, they more often than not find themselves in the right place. They have a way of making the game look easy.

In this section we will analyze proper throwing techniques, discuss fielding ground balls and fly balls, delve into each position in the infield and outfield, and break down double plays and relay situations.

You will learn that balance, anticipation, alertness, aggressiveness, footwork, technique, quickness, and concentration are key characteristics of the skilled defensive player. Each of these qualities is critical in the development of young players, and they should learn early how to catch, field, and throw properly. The ability of the defensive player to maintain balance will determine his consistency, his ability to make the great play, and ultimately the level of his success. Proper footwork and quick hands and feet allow players to play at the faster pace the game requires as they climb the ladder in baseball. The ability to focus, concentrate, and truly want each swing to send the ball his way will help the player as much as anything.

Anything a player can do to improve his arm strength and accuracy, agility, quickness, speed, comfort level, and confidence through repetition will help him succeed. In this section we will give you some ideas about how to improve the skills of your players through techniques and drills. Players should pay attention, read and process the information, and above all, practice. Coaches should expect perfect practice from their players.

Throwing

Throwing is an essential skill for both infielders and outfielders. Infielders obviously have to make more throws and more different types of throws than outfielders, but outfielders must be able to make long, accurate, and timely throws. The skill of throwing can catch the eye of a recruiter, allow the player to play more positions on the field, enable him to make more difficult plays, and can save the game in tough situations.

Learning how to throw from different angles with accuracy, consistency, and velocity will give the player the versatility to handle different positions and situations. Each position and each situation requires a different type of throw and a different adjustment to the throwing motion. The mechanics of throwing are basic to most of the throws needed. This chapter will address the fundamental mechanics.

Through many years of experience, I have found that drills and better mechanics can vastly improve and develop players' throwing strength and accuracy. If a player works 20 to 30 minutes a day on his throwing, he will see significant improvement. As a coach arrives at the ballpark to evaluate players, one with a strong arm always jumps out at him. The coach is sure to watch him further.

Size and strength contribute to throwing ability, but I have seen small players with quick arms outthrow larger, stronger players. This leads me to believe that throwing is a specific skill and that with proper repetitions, technique, and concentration, almost everyone has the ability to become a strong thrower. Throwing is one skill that a player can improve significantly through hard work and proper teaching.

In this chapter, we will talk about the basic mechanics of throwing and suggest some drills to develop a stronger, more accurate arm.

Figure 6.1 Right-handed thrower moving through the ball to catch.

THROWING MECHANICS

In starting to outline throwing mechanics, we should note a couple of elements that are required for good throwing technique. First, in preparing to throw it is almost always necessary for the player to move through the ball toward the target. When players are playing catch, I like to see them move through the ball, stepping with the left foot, for a right-handed thrower, to the ball (figure 6.1).

The second important element is that after receiving the ball, the player starts to take it directly to the area of the throwing shoulder. At that time, the throwing side foot turns perpendicularly to the target, similar to the way a pitcher pivots on the rubber. A flex and bend in the legs help with balance, lowering the center of gravity and allowing the legs to become a part of the power of the throw.

The First 90 Percent: Preparing to Throw

After receiving the ball, the player determines the purpose, time, and distance of the throw he will use to make the play. These elements will determine the arc of the throwing arm. By grabbing the ball across the seams, the player ensures that the ball will travel in a straighter path with greater accuracy, speed, and distance.

Checklist for Preparing to Throw

- The elbows stay up.
- The hands are together about midchest.
- The player pivots on the throwing foot and aligns the chin, lead elbow, lead hip, outside of the lead knee, and outside of the lead heel toward the target.
- He takes the ball out of the glove with two fingers of the throwing hand placed across the seams and on top of the ball.
- The throwing arm moves back through the desired arc. Remember, the longer the throw and the more time the player has, the longer the arc of the throwing arm. The shorter the throw and the less time he has, the shorter the arc of the throwing arm.
- The lead-arm thumb extends downward.
- The player moves the throwing arm forward toward the release point and moves the lead arm back toward the chest.

At this point, the player must align several checkpoints toward his target. The player is trying to store up all his energy before releasing the ball. To do this, he must transfer the ball, keep his elbows up from his midchest area to his shoulders, and keep his hands together to about the middle of his chest as he pivots to throw (figure 6.2a). By using this technique, the player stays more compact, stores up his energy, and maintains better balance. A player who drops or raises his elbows, breaks his hands early, and spreads out will lose accuracy and velocity and may later develop arm problems. The longer the throw and the more time he has, the longer the arc of the throwing arm. The shorter the throw and the less time he has, the shorter the arc.

As he pivots on his throwing foot, the player aligns his chin, lead elbow, lead hip, outside of the lead knee, and outside of the lead heel toward the target (figure 6.2b). The ball comes out of the glove with two fingers of the throwing hand across the seams and on top of the ball. The ball moves back away from the player through the desired arc. The front arm extends thumb down toward the target in a semiflexed position as the throwing arm moves to the top of the arc. As the throwing arm moves forward toward the release point, the lead arm draws back inward toward the lead side of the chest (figure 6.2c). The longer the throw and the more time he has, the longer the arc of the throwing arm. The shorter the throw and the less time he has, the shorter the arc.

The Last 10 Percent: Releasing the Ball

At this point, the upper body leans forward toward the target as the throwing hand nears the release point. The throw is 90 percent complete, but the last 10 percent makes the difference. The release of the ball (the last 10 percent of the throw, as I call it) is a loose-to-firm release. This critical part of the throw controls the final accuracy

a   b   c

Figure 6.2 Elements of the first 90% of a throw. *(a)* The player keeps the elbow up and the hands together at midchest while pivoting to throw. *(b)* The player pivots on the throwing foot with the chin, elbow, hip, outside of knee, and outside of heel aligned to the target. *(c)* As the lead arm retreats, the throwing arm moves forward to the release point.

and velocity of the ball. The ball is released off the index and middle fingers with much backspin, which gives the ball true flight and carry toward the target.

I use the term "nose to leather" to describe the emphasis the player should put on following the flight of his throw after release. The player watches the completion of the throw by sticking his nose and eyes on the target until it hits the leather of the receiver (figure 6.3).

Early release from the nose-to-leather technique will affect accuracy and weaken the flight of the ball.

A former pitcher at Clemson University named Kris Benson made me a believer in the last 10 percent of the throw and the nose-to-leather idea. Kris came to school

Checklist for Releasing the Ball

- Lean the upper body forward toward the target as the throwing hand approaches the release point.
- Execute a loose-to-firm release of the ball. Release the ball off the index and middle fingers with backspin.
- Follow the flight of the throw, nose to leather.

throwing 85 to 86 miles per hour. As a junior, he threw 93 to 95 miles per hour. Through strength training, solid mechanics, and an emphasis on the finish of his throws, Kris became college baseball's top player and the number-one selection in the 1996 draft. His last 10 percent and his concentration on the flight of the ball to the leather helped make him the great major-league pitcher he is today.

THROWING DRILLS

Many drills can improve throwing technique and strength, but I will narrow them down to my seven favorites. Players should do these drills daily. Anything a player can do to work on flexibility and strength in his legs, shoulders, midsection, forearms, wrists, hands, and fingers will help him put more force on the ball and create more velocity. Strength and flexibility training will also help prevent injury and take pressure off the joints and surrounding muscles. Players should follow a comprehensive stretching and weightlifting program year round.

Figure 6.3 Nose-to-leather follow-through.

The following drills specifically address the throwing mechanics necessary for improvement. After elevating his temperature by running and stretching, and after executing the first six drills in the following sequence, players should perform a consistent long-throwing pattern for about 20 to 30 minutes each day. Depending on how his arm feels, the player can shorten or lengthen the throwing distance.

Cross-Legged Sitting Drill

Purpose: To reinforce the ball rotation needed for accuracy and carry.

Procedure:
1. Partners sit cross-legged on the ground, 10 to 15 feet apart, facing each other.
2. One player holds the ball across the seams with his forearm perpendicular to the ground and his throwing elbow about shoulder height (figure 6.4a). With his opposite hand, he holds his throwing elbow.
3. As he moves his throwing forearm forward, he tries to accentuate the backspin and four-seam rotation (figure 6.4b).

Coaching Points: Check the four-seam grip and proper rotation of the ball, and emphasize the last 10 percent of the throw as a reminder and as a way to develop the finish.

a   b

Figure 6.4   Cross-Legged Sitting drill.

Two-Knee Throwing Drill

Purpose: To emphasize proper upper-body throwing technique and the importance of the last 10 percent.

Procedure:

1. Partners kneel on both knees on the ground facing each other about 20 to 30 feet apart. (You can adjust the distance according to the arm strength and age of the players; as they become more proficient, you can move them farther apart.)

2. As the player throws, he concentrates on upper-body mechanics by
   - holding his hands together to the midline of his chest as he rotates to point his front shoulder at his partner (figure 6.5a),
   - keeping his elbows at chest level,
   - holding his chest upright, and
   - fixing his eyes on the target.

3. As the player breaks his hands and executes the throw, he drives the throwing arm forward with fluid quickness, emphasizing the last 10 percent and strong four-seam rotation (figure 6.5b).

4. Players move farther apart as they warm up and begin to throw with more intensity. They execute 15 to 30 throws before moving to the next drill.

Coaching Points: Players must never sacrifice proper technique for distance. During warm-ups, this drill becomes an aggressive throwing drill with players snapping the throws. Only then does the drill reach maximum effectiveness.

a   b

Figure 6.5   Two-Knee Throwing drill.

One-Knee Throwing Drill

This drill is similar to the Two-Knee Throwing drill except that the lead leg is extended in front.

Purpose: To reinforce upper-body mechanics, with an emphasis on extending over the lead leg.

Procedure:
1. Partners face each other about 20 to 30 feet apart. (You can adjust the distance according to arm strength and age; as players become more proficient, you can increase the distance.)
2. Players kneel on the throwing-hand-side knee with the lead leg forward. The lead foot should not extend past the lead knee (figure 6.6a). This positioning will allow the player to extend over the front side toward the target when he throws (figure 6.6b).
3. As the player throws, he concentrates on upper-body mechanics by
   • holding his hands together to the midline of his chest as he rotates to point his front shoulder at his partner,
   • keeping his elbows at chest level,
   • holding his chest upright, and
   • fixing his eyes on the target.

a   b

Figure 6.6 One-Knee Throwing drill.

4. As the player breaks his hands and executes the throw, he drives the throwing arm forward with fluid quickness, emphasizing the last 10 percent and strong four-seam rotation.

5. Players move farther apart as they warm up and begin to throw with more intensity. They execute 15 to 30 throws before moving to the next drill.

Coaching Points: Make sure that players use proper upper-body mechanics. They should concentrate on easy arm action and great extension toward the target, releasing the ball in front of the lead leg. You can increase the distance as the players become stronger throwers.

Ten Toes Drill

Purpose: To reinforce proper weight and energy transfer through the body.

Procedure:
1. Partners stand and face each other. The knees are slightly flexed to help with balance and the transfer of energy from the ground up through the rest of the body. The feet are shoulder-width apart.

2. The upper-body mechanics are the same as those used in the Two-Knee Throwing drill and the One-Knee Throwing drill (figure 6.7a).

3. The thrower aims at his partner's chest, concentrating on proper weight transfer through the body, correct upper-body mechanics, and an aggressive last 10 percent (figure 6.7b).

4. The distance and number of throws varies according to the players' conditioning level.

a   b

Figure 6.7 Ten Toes drill.

Coaching Points: With the knees bent, players will realize the importance of the lower body in throwing the ball. This drill helps the player understand how the lower half and upper half of the body work together in throwing.

Ten Toes–Figure-8 Drill

This drill is performed in the same manner as the Ten Toes drill, except that it starts with a rhythmical figure-8 movement with the upper body.

Purpose: To teach and reinforce rhythm and flow in throwing.

Procedure:
1. Partners stand and face each other. The knees are slightly flexed to help with balance and the transfer of energy from the ground up through the rest of the body. The feet are shoulder-width apart.
2. The upper-body mechanics are the same as those used in the Two-Knee Throwing drill and the One-Knee Throwing drill.
3. The thrower begins the drill by executing a figure-8 movement. For the figure-8 movement, the player holds his hands together and rotates them from the left side of his body (figure 6.8a) to the right side (figure 6.8b). As he moves his hands in the figure 8, he keeps his hands above the belt.

4. After two to three figure 8s, the thrower aims at his partner's chest, concentrating on proper weight transfer through the body, proper upper-body mechanics, and an aggressive last 10 percent (figure 6.8c).

5. The distance and number of throws varies according to the players' conditioning level.

a   b   c

Figure 6.8 Ten Toes–Figure-8 drill.

Coaching Points: It is important that players stay loose during the figure-8 movement and learn to develop rhythm in throwing. Emphasize that they must keep the hands together so that they can stay compact during execution of the throw.

Walking Figure-8 Drill

This drill is similar to the previous drill except now the partners walk toward each other as they execute the figure-8 movement.

Purpose: To enhance throwing rhythm, reinforce the importance of keeping the hands together to stay compact, and practice proper throwing technique and motion.

Procedure:

1. Partners stand approximately 60 feet apart and face each other. (You can increase the distance to 120 feet, depending on players' skill level and conditioning.)

2. The upper-body mechanics are the same as those used in the Two-Knee Throwing drill and the One-Knee Throwing drill.

3. The thrower begins the drill by executing a figure-8 movement with his hands together. He walks toward his partner as he performs the figure 8s (figure 6.9a).

4. He flexes his knees and keeps his hands together to emphasize staying compact. After two to three figure 8s, the thrower aims at his partner's chest (figure 6.9b), concentrating on proper weight transfer through the body, correct upper-body mechanics, and an aggressive last 10 percent (figure 6.9c).

5. After throwing the ball, the thrower returns to his original spot.

6. Players execute the drill 20 to 30 times.

a   b   c

Figure 6.9 Walking Figure-8 drill.

Coaching Points: Walking toward a partner while executing the figure 8 helps develop rhythm and puts movement and rhythm together in the throwing motion. Players should stay loose throughout the body and stay compact while executing the figure-8 movement.

Long-Toss Drill

Purpose: To increase arm strength and endurance and improve accuracy and concentration.

Procedure:

1. Partners begin 50 feet apart, standing and facing each other.

2. They play catch, executing 5 to 10 throws before stepping back. They move back in 15- to 20-foot increments until they are 250 to 300 feet apart, depending on arm strength and conditioning.

3. After 10 to 20 throws at maximum distance, the players begin to move closer together and flatten out the arc. They make their throws more direct and execute at full velocity at distances of 150 feet, 120 feet, 110 feet, and 60 feet.

4. By now, the players should be very warm and loose. They should work on this drill after doing the previous drills, and they can lengthen or shorten the throwing pattern based on how their arms feel.

Coaching Points: At maximum distance, the arc of the throw should never be greater than 45 degrees. We have had players at Clemson who could throw the ball from home plate over the 328 sign. Only through a long-throwing program will a player have a chance to develop this type of arm strength.

7

Fielding Ground Balls

Courtesy of Clemson University

In this chapter, we will deal with the technique and thought process that will help young infielders become more successful. To improve his fielding skills, an infielder must be able to concentrate, must be aggressive, and must be willing to practice. Only through correct repetition can an infielder develop the confidence and attitude necessary to be the best. After an infielder has practiced enough, he will want the ball to come his way on every pitch and in any situation. Slick-fielding infielders jump out at you when you watch a game, and a coach can tell which infielders have invested the time to build their skills.

We will talk about five basic types of ground balls and the keys to fielding them correctly. These ground balls are

- the ground ball hit directly at the infielder,
- the ground ball hit to the glove-hand side,
- the V-cut ground ball,
- the ground ball hit to the backhand side, and
- the slow-roller ground ball.

Before we discuss each ground ball, it is important to understand some basic principles to fielding each of them. The player should

- be aggressive and attack the ball,
- be under control,
- create an angle toward the throwing target,
- always work toward balance,
- look the ball into the glove,
- stay low with the ball,
- remember that after fielding the ball, the job is only half done, and
- stay compact when throwing and follow the nose-to-leather idea explained in the chapter on throwing.

With any ground ball the player should know several things ahead of time so that he can make better decisions on his approach to the ball:

- The type and condition of the surface he is playing on
- The speed of the hitter and runners, if any
- The position of the runners on base
- The number of outs
- The score of the game
- The inning
- The type of pitcher he is playing behind, the count, and the type of pitch being thrown
- His own strengths and limitations

The infielder should understand the need to be aggressive and to attack the ball under control to shorten up the distance of the throw. A good infielder also creates an angle to shorten the throwing distance and improve accuracy and strength on the throw.

An infielder who takes a lot of ground balls knows that he needs to field the ball on one of three hops:

1. at the top of the hop,
2. on the down side of the hop, or
3. on the short hop.

He must gauge his angles and aggressiveness to field one of these hops and avoid the up hop. The up hop hits the ground, picks up top spin, and is on the way up past the short hop–phase. Some people call this the in-between hop. Repetition, little spurts of acceleration, and extension of the hands toward the ball are ways to avoid the up hop.

One of the most important concepts is that the fielder should play the ball and not let it play him. He almost always moves toward the ball even if he has to move only slightly on a hard-hit ball. Another important concept is to create an angle. The infielder does this by moving slightly from right to left through the ball as he approaches and fields it. Another key point is to stay low. The eyes, body position, and glove should stay near the height of the bounces. By using this positioning and by keeping the eyes still and level, the fielder can more easily judge the bouncing ball.

Now that we have established some guidelines, let's move to the specific techniques for fielding the ball hit directly at the infielder. Note that all of the explanations on technique describe the movements of a right-handed-throwing infielder.

FIELDING THE GROUND BALL HIT DIRECTLY AT THE FIELDER

All infielders should start by mastering the ground ball hit directly at them. The technique involved is the basis for fielding all other types of ground balls. The ball hit right at a player poses some unique challenges:

- It is tougher for the player to judge the speed of a ball hit at him than one hit off to the side.
- It is more difficult for the player to judge the distance of the bounces when the ball is coming at him.
- Players have a tendency to come up out of their positions, and they then must lower themselves to field the ball.
- Players tend to freeze and let the ball play them.

To field the ball hit right at him, the infielder walks into his stance with a right-left step and then a controlled hop step. The timing of the hop should coincide with the arrival of the pitched ball in the hitting zone. The glove should be open to the ball with the glove-hand elbow inward, which will allow the palm to be more open (figure 7.1). The fielder should have the knees bent, arms semiflexed in front, and feet about shoulder-width apart. Players just starting out should use a very low stance to become accustomed to working from the ground up. Advanced players who understand the fielding concepts can start higher to increase their range.

As the ball is hit, the fielder moves to it, stepping with the right foot first to start creating an angle toward the target at first base. He approaches the ball with his eyes still and low with the ball. The hands should be in front of the body with the palm of the glove open to the ball.

Figure 7.1 The glove is open to the ball as the pitch is thrown.

The player readies himself to field the ball on the top of the hop, on the down hop, or on the short hop. Fielding the ball off the glove-hand eye, he extends the glove out in front and underneath the ball with the throwing hand over the top of the ball (figure 7.2a). His knees are bent and his butt is down so that he can extend the hands. Only then will he be able to create soft hands. His feet should be almost perpendicular to the direction the ball is coming from and a little wider than shoulder-width apart.

Just before contact with the ball, the hands give with the ball. The right hand closes over the top of the ball as contact is made with the glove out in front of the glove-hand eye. (The eyes follow the ball into the glove.) Using two hands, the fielder brings the ball to his belt buckle or the center of his body (figure 7.2b). Young players need to focus on doing this to achieve balance.

The feet replace themselves or the right foot crosses in front of the left to gain distance toward the target and add momentum to the throw. As this is happening, the hands move the ball to the throwing shoulder (figure 7.2c). The fielder throws the ball and observes the nose-to-leather technique.

a

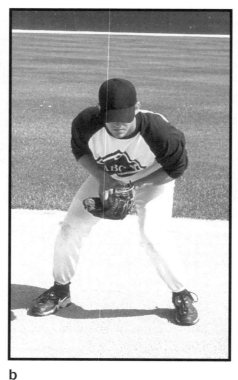

b

c

Figure 7.2 Fielding the ground ball. *(a)* The glove extends under the ball as the throwing hand closes over the ball. *(b)* The ball is brought to the center of the body. *(c)* As the right foot crosses in front of the left foot, the ball is moved to the throwing shoulder.

FIELDING THE GROUND BALL HIT TO THE GLOVE-HAND SIDE

Of the five basic ground balls, I consider the ball on the glove-hand side the easiest to field for several reasons. First, in most cases, the ball takes the fielder closer to the target. Second, it is a bit easier to judge the speed and distance of the hops when the ball is hit slightly off to the side. Third, the fielder can put a little momentum into his throws.

As the fielder walks into his stance and the batter hits the ball, the fielder crosses over with his right foot and determines the most direct path to the ball that will allow him to field it on one of his three favorite hops (figure 7.3). The fielder's angle should be as direct and aggressive as possible because the hitter gains ground toward first base with every step the fielder takes toward the ball.

The fielder should move after the ground ball with his eyes as low as possible, the palm of his glove open to the ball, and his glove carried around knee level and slightly out in front of his right knee (figure 7.4a).

The infielder accelerates and attacks to field the ball on the top of the hop, on the down hop, or on the short hop. If possible, he fields the ball using the same principles he used with the ball hit right at him:

1. He fields out to in.
2. He fields down to up.
3. He fields off the glove-hand eye.
4. He takes the ball into the stomach and then to the shoulder.
5. He points the front shoulder to the target and replaces the feet or crosses over in front (figure 7.4b).
6. He finishes the throw with the nose-to-leather technique

Figure 7.3 Crossing with his right foot, the fielder determines the most direct path to the ball.

Figure 7.4 Fielding the ground ball hit to the glove-hand side. *(a)* Once he gets to the ball, the fielder fields it as if it were hit right to him. *(b)* After fielding the ball, the fielder turns his front shoulder to point to the target and brings the ball to his throwing shoulder.

a

b

If the ball is hit far to the glove-hand side and the fielder must extend himself to field it outside his left foot with one hand, he must make a few adjustments. As he fields the ball, he aggressively takes it to his throwing shoulder to meet his throwing hand. His upper body bends slightly at the waist and leans back in the direction he came from. He does this to slow his momentum and maintain balance. The right foot passes back behind the left foot to provide stability for the throw.

The fielder should try to throw the ball with his arm parallel to the ground or at a three-quarter-arm angle. This technique will ensure better accuracy and put less tail on the ball. The fielder should lock on to his target after throwing, watching as the ball contacts the leather.

FIELDING THE V-CUT GROUND BALL

Fielding a slowly hit ground ball on the backhand side is a difficult play. The ball moves the infielder away from his target, requiring him to move back through it when fielding so that he can develop some momentum and shorten the distance of the throw. Some people call the approach to this kind of hit "rounding the ball off." I use the term V-cut because it signifies a more aggressive approach to the ball.

As the ball is hit toward the backhand side, the fielder crosses over with the left foot and then decides that the ball is not hit hard enough or far enough for him to backhand it. Realizing this, the fielder aggressively attacks the ball and moves his feet with quick steps to a spot beyond the path of the ball (figure 7.5a). He plants hard on his right foot, which helps his body move back toward his throwing target. His eyes remain low with the glove in front of his body (figure 7.5b). As he moves

a b c

Figure 7.5 Fielding the V-cut ground ball. *(a)* The fielder quickly moves to a spot beyond the ball. *(b)* He plants on his right foot, keeping his glove in front. *(c)* He crosses his right foot in front of his left, creating a straight angle to the target.

through the ball in fielding it, he can field the ball in the center of the body or slightly to the throwing-hand eye. This is a do-or-die ground ball that he must field and release quickly. After fielding the ball, the glove, ball, and hands move quickly to the throwing shoulder. The right foot crosses in front of the left to prepare for the throw and create a straight angle to the target (figure 7.5c). He throws, follows his throw, and sticks the "nose to the leather."

BACKHANDING THE BALL

The ability to make the backhand play consistently is what separates the great player from the good players. This play challenges a fielder's athletic ability, footwork, balance, and throwing arm. To execute the play, the player must practice a great deal and have excellent arm strength.

A ball that the fielder needs to backhand is usually hit hard and traveling fast. Therefore, the fielder again performs the crossover step, moving the left foot in front of the right foot as he starts after the ball. He decides that he will have to backhand the ball rather than use the V-cut approach.

The fielder should move low to the ball, trying to take a straight path to field it on one of the three favorable hops. Time is of the essence because he is moving away from the target and he will have to make a long throw.

By approaching the ball with his knees bent, the fielder's eyes are closer to the ball. He should try to keep his eyes level to the ground so that he can better judge the bounces. As the fielder approaches the fielding point, his left elbow turns out, his glove thumb rotates down, and the fingers inside his glove spread to make the glove as wide as possible (figure 7.6a).

At maximum extension, the fielder can field the ball 6 to 18 inches in front of his glove-hand foot. He swipes into the ball slightly so that he fields it deeper in the pocket, which will help him prepare for the throw. As the fielder moves into the ball with his glove, his fingers start to close to secure the ball. The right foot travels around the back of the glove, and the player plants hard on the inside cleats of his right foot. His right knee should be inside his foot and should not drift over the foot (figure 7.6b). This positioning will help the player establish a strong plant leg for the throw. As the player plants his right foot, the glove and hands move directly to the throwing shoulder.

At this point, the fielder starts the throw. A few key principles are important here. The fielder should open up his front hip slightly when throwing to eliminate

a

b

Figure 7.6 Backhanding the ground ball. (a) The fielder approaches the fielding point. (b) He plants his right foot, with his right knee to the inside of his foot.

tail on the ball and ensure better accuracy. He needs to throw the ball over the top from a high angle to help the ball carry better toward the target. He then must follow his throw by moving his body, after the release, toward the target. A nose-to-leather approach is vital here.

FIELDING THE SLOW-ROLLER GROUND BALL

This ground ball requires an aggressive attack by the fielder. The play requires athleticism and balance, the ability to throw on the run, and an understanding of how to create an angle to make the play easier. Most of the time a slow roller is created by a bunt, a chopped ball, a topped ball, a swing by a batter who is jammed by a pitch, or a swing that hits the ball on the end of the bat. The fielder can make the play more intelligently if he knows the speed of the hitter and is familiar with the type of surface he is playing on.

One-Handed Method

To field the slow roller, the player must first create an angle toward his target while attacking the ball aggressively. If the fielder steps first with his right foot on the way to the ball and then approaches the ball slightly from right to left, he will be in better position to field and throw the ball. He should approach the ball with the palm of his glove open and with the glove in front of his body and near thigh level. His eyes should remain as calm and level as possible to avoid having to field a bouncing ball with bouncing eyes (figure 7.7a).

The fielder bends his knees as he readies himself to field the ball. He fields the ball one handed by swinging slightly through the ball with the glove. This action saves time and starts the glove and ball moving to the center of the body. He fields the ball just outside the left foot (figure 7.7b). As the player starts to bring his hands with the ball to the middle of his body, he starts to become more upright with his upper body (figure 7.7c). At this time, he transfers his weight to his right foot. The left foot comes forward as the hands start to break. At the same time, the fielder angles toward his target on the run. As the right foot lands, the throwing arm is set to throw at a position parallel to the ground or higher. The fielder has extended the glove hand out for balance, and he then pulls it back aggressively to the left side of the chest as he releases the ball, throwing off the right leg (figure 7.7d). His belt buckle should face the target and he should throw the ball slightly to the left of the target to allow for some tail on the ball. The fielder should follow his throw and watch the ball into the glove of his teammate.

Two-Handed Method

Players should also learn the two-handed fielding method (figure 7.8). The approach is the same but the ball is fielded with two hands 6 to 18 inches inside and in front of the throwing-hand foot. The fielder brings the ball up to the waist as he plants the left foot. The hands break, the throwing arm moves to throw, and the glove moves out and back to the left side of the chest as the right foot plants. Brooks Robinson was the best I ever saw at the slow roller, but his two-step technique is tough to master. He fielded the ball on the inside of his left foot and transferred it quickly to the throwing area as he planted his right foot. He delivered the ball in two steps.

a

b

c

d

Figure 7.7 Fielding a slow-rolling ground ball with one hand. *(a)* The fielder keeps his eyes level. *(b)* He nabs the ball slightly to the outside of his left foot. *(c)* He brings the ball to mid-body and stands more upright. *(d)* He moves his glove hand back toward his chest as he releases the ball off his right leg.

Figure 7.8 The two-handed fielding method.

I have found that most young players need the extra step when fielding the ball with two hands. I see the value of the one-handed fielding technique because it allows the fielder to approach the ball aggressively, requires less flexibility, and allows for a harder throw to first base in most cases.

GROUND-BALL DRILLS

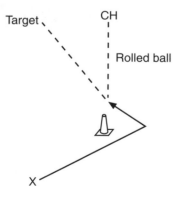

Figure 7.9 Setup for the V-Cut drill.

V-Cut Drill

Purpose: To emphasize the fielding angle needed for fielding a V-cut ground ball.

Procedure:
1. Place a cone, ball, or glove in front and to the right of the fielder (figure 7.9).
2. Roll a ball toward the fielder. He must move his feet quickly around the cone, field the ball, and throw to a target.

Coaching Points: The fielder should be aggressive with his feet and exaggerate his movement beyond the cone so that he fields the ball moving sharply toward the target.

Clap Drill

This drill breaks the skill down step by step.

Purpose: To practice fielding the backhand ball, regaining balance, and getting to the throwing position quickly.

Procedure:
1. The player bends to field an imaginary ball to the backhand side.
2. After swiping through the imaginary ball, he plants his right foot hard and claps his hands at the throwing slot.

Coaching Points: The player will learn the quickness and balance it takes to field a backhand ground ball. He stays low and executes three or four consecutive swipe-to-clap imaginary ground balls. One step, swipe, plant, clap—it's a four-step drill.

8

Fielding Fly Balls

n this chapter, we will analyze the most effective techniques for fielding fly balls. Although we will talk mostly about how an outfielder approaches the ball, the information applies to any player fielding a fly ball. Figure 8.1 shows the priorities on fly balls and the fielders' approximate areas in our fly-ball scheme.

Communication and teamwork are critical in fielding fly balls, but ultimately success depends on the player's proper execution. We will start with the ready position, the thought process in being ready, and the footwork and glove work needed to be successful.

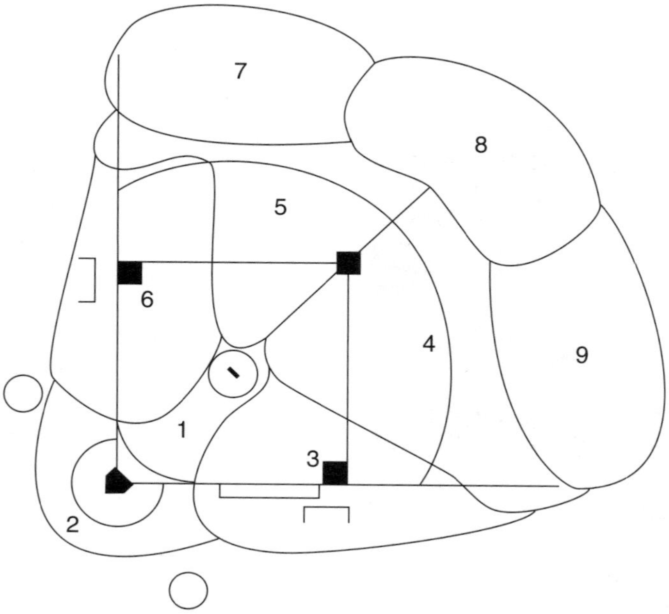

With respect to the position of the outfielder, fly balls are hit to five locations:

1. at the outfielder,
2. to the glove-hand side,
3. to the throwing-hand side,
4. behind the outfielder, and
5. in front of the outfielder.

To field fly balls properly, the outfielder should have knowledge of the hitter, the pitch being thrown, the field dimensions, the weather conditions, and the game situation.

Figure 8.1 Fly ball fielding zones.

FIELDING THE FLY BALL HIT AT THE FIELDER

The fielder should walk into his stance in a way similar to how an infielder prepares to field a ground ball, with a right-left step and a slight hop. He should time his walk as the ball enters the hitting zone. His knees should be slightly flexed with his upper body leaning forward only slightly and his glove just in front of his glove-side hip (figure 8.2).

When the ball is hit in his direction, the fielder turns his feet and body a half turn to his glove side (figure 8.3). He evaluates the direction, speed, and depth of the ball. He locks his eyes on the ball. Once he gets a read on the ball and realizes that it is hit right at him, the fielder moves backward slightly by crossing his feet. His shoulders are still parallel to the ball as he prepares himself to get back behind the ball. As the ball starts to descend, the fielder squares his shoulders to the ball and lightly shuffles his feet, moving into the ball with his glove about chin high and the palm of his glove close to a 45-degree angle to the downward flight of the ball. His throwing hand is slightly lower and off to the side.

The fielder times his catch so that as he fields the ball he steps forward with his glove-side foot (figure 8.4). He catches the ball with his glove as high as the top of his head, stepping into the ball with his glove-side foot. Fielding the ball with two hands is strongly encouraged. Upon receiving the ball, he brings the ball in front of his face across to his throwing side, chest high.

The fielder then steps through and forward with his throwing foot and pivots sideways, or perpendicularly, to the intended target (figure 8.5). This enables him

Figure 8.2 Ready position—knees slightly flexed, upper body leaning forward, and glove in front of hip.

Figure 8.3 The fielder makes a half turn to his glove side.

Figure 8.4 The fielder steps forward with his glove-side foot.

Figure 8.5 The fielder steps forward with his throwing foot, pivoting sideways to the target.

to get into the proper throwing position and line up his front shoulder to the target. The outfielder should throw over the top so that the throw will stay straight and carry farther. He should follow through to the target and stay on the throw until he sees the ball make contact with the glove of his relay man.

FIELDING THE FLY BALL HIT TO THE GLOVE-HAND SIDE

After walking into his stance, the fielder reacts to the ball on his glove side by taking a short jab step to his glove side. His lead foot opens at a 45-degree angle, and his initiated path is close to a 45-degree angle rather than a straight path to the glove side (figure 8.6). After opening up, the fielder crosses his feet over on each stride. It is always easier to adjust to the ball when moving in rather than moving back. The player should move smoothly to ensure that his eyes are still. He should carry his glove as if running without it and extend it only when he is ready to field the ball. Extending the glove arm too soon will slow him down. If he must field the fly ball on the run one handed, he should extend his glove at the last moment to make the catch.

If the fly ball is not hit so far to the glove side that it requires a one-handed catch, the fielder should position himself behind the ball and move through it as he makes the catch. He keeps his chest and shoulders square to the ball (figure 8.7). The player uses the same fielding technique that he used for fielding fly balls hit right at him.

Figure 8.6 The fielder takes a jab step to his glove side, opening his lead foot to a 45-degree angle.

Figure 8.7 The fielder positions himself behind the ball.

FIELDING THE FLY BALL HIT TO THE THROWING SIDE

To field a fly ball hit to the throwing side, the fielder uses the same preliminary movements that he used with other fly balls. On contact by the hitter, the fielder takes an open jab step with his throwing-side foot (figure 8.8). He approaches the ball in a way similar to how he approaches a ball hit to his glove-hand side, only now he turns his wrist over with his thumb down and spreads his fingers in the glove to catch the fly ball on the run (figure 8.9).

If it is not necessary to field the ball on the run, the fielder should run to the spot where he can get behind the ball, square his chest and shoulders to it, and make the catch using the same technique he uses for the ball hit right at him.

Figure 8.8 The fielder takes a jab step with his throwing-side foot.

Figure 8.9 The fielder turns over his wrist, points the thumb down, and spreads his fingers.

FIELDING THE FLY BALL HIT OVERHEAD

The player prepares the same way he did for other fly balls by walking into his stance and then taking a little hop step as the hitter is about to make contact. When the fielder realizes the ball has been hit directly over his head, he shifts to the side to locate the ball and determine its speed and depth. Left and right fielders normally open up and face the foul lines because the ball will most likely tail to the lines. (A right-handed hitter will hook the ball slightly to left field and slice the ball to right field. A left-handed hitter will do the opposite.)

As the fielder pivots to the side, his back foot opens up slightly more than 90 degrees. We call this "opening the gate" (figure 8.10). The fielder should try to keep his eyes on the ball, but occasionally he must just turn and run to where he predicts the ball will fall.

FIELDING THE SHALLOW FLY BALL HIT IN FRONT OF THE FIELDER

Upon contact by the hitter, the fielder reacts to the ball hit in front of him by taking a quick drop step with either his left or right foot (figure 8.11). The fielder heads toward the short fly ball with steady eyes and runs on the balls of his feet. He carries his glove hand as if he were running without it, but as he nears the ball he should gradually work his hands in front of his body; keeping his palm up and elbow down (figure 8.12). Only as a last option should he turn the glove under the ball.

Figure 8.10 Opening the gate.

Figure 8.11 At contact, the fielder drop steps back.

Figure 8.12 The fielder prepares to receive the ball.

FLY-BALL DRILLS

Short-Distance Fly Balls off the Ponza Machine

Purpose: To break down the technique, angles, footwork, and receiving position of the outfielder in a smaller area. The drill emphasizes taking the correct route to the ball and making the catch properly.

Procedure:
1. The fielder walks into his stance and waits for the ball.
2. The coach uses the Ponza machine to send the fielder each type of fly ball (fly ball hit at him, hit to the glove-hand side, hit to the throwing-hand side, hit behind him, and hit in front of him).
3. The outfielder moves to field each type of fly ball sent by the machine. The fielder takes the correct angle and uses the right footwork to execute the catch.
4. After catching the fly ball, the fielder returns the ball using proper technique to a relay man.

Coaching Points: Emphasize to the fielder that he must take the proper first step, move at the correct angle to the ball, and position himself to throw as he catches the ball. Use many repetitions to create good habits and sound fundamentals.

Agility Footwork to Enhance Balance

Purpose: To improve the outfielder's footwork and force him to make adjustments in starting his route to the ball.

Procedure:
1. The outfielder stands in ready position facing the coach.
2. The fielder scissors his feet as if doing an agility drill. The coach throws the ball to an area that will challenge the fielder to move and catch the ball on balance.
3. After fielding the ball on balance, the fielder throws to a base.

Coaching Points: By having to move his feet quickly in place in a scissor motion, the outfielder is forced to make a quick adjustment in preparing himself to hustle after the ball.

Fielding Fly Balls and Throwing to Bases

Purpose: To teach outfielders to field fly balls and quickly take proper position to throw to bases.

Procedure:
1. The right fielder, center fielder, and left fielder assume their correct positions in the outfield.
2. A batter or coach hits long fly balls to the outfielders. The fielders must use proper footwork, angles, glove position, and preparation to field the ball and throw to a base.
3. After fielding the fly ball, the outfielder throws to an infielder at second base, third base, or home plate. You can vary the base depending on the theme for that practice.

Coaching Points: This drill enhances the outfielder's ability to throw to bases after fielding a fly ball. Emphasize taking proper angles to the ball, using correct fielding position, and moving through the ball to throw to a base. Also note throwing mechanics, accuracy, and carry on the ball to the intended base.

Fielding Positions 3 Through 9

In this chapter, we will discuss some of the characteristics and responsibilities of the infield and outfield positions. Each position requires a certain type of athlete who is proficient at special skills. To be a strong defensive player at his position, a fielder must always be alert, must know the situation, and must communicate with the fielders around him. We all know players who set the standard for each position, and young players should try to emulate them.

Proper positioning allows each player to make the plays that will help his team win. Players should position themselves with several things in mind. The following factors will determine the depth and lateral position of the fielders:

- the type of hitter (pull or opposite field);
- the hitter's capabilities (bunter or nonbunter, speed);
- the type of pitcher throwing and the type of pitch being thrown;
- the situation (score, number of outs, inning, and count);
- the weather conditions (wet, windy);
- the type of playing surface (artificial turf, high grass, short grass);
- the speed of the hitter and the speed of the runners on base;
- the other runners on base, if any (man on first, double-play possibility, man on second, man on third); and, most important,
- the strengths and weaknesses of the fielder himself.

INFIELDERS

The infield will go a long way in determining the success of your team. How well they communicate, how well they work together, how athletic they are, and how skilled they are will make the difference in their effectiveness. Infielders who complement each other, who can make the routine plays, turn the double play, handle all situations that may occur, and come up with great plays when necessary can take their teams to championships. As a group, they must communicate and exhibit leadership.

First Baseman

Your first baseman should be aggressive and athletic, with agile feet and excellent hands. A good knowledge of the game and situations is helpful because the first baseman is involved in a variety of plays. A first baseman on the taller side can be a better target for the other infielders. In my years of coaching, I've had excellent right-handed first basemen as well as outstanding left-handed first basemen. I don't have a preference, as long as my first baseman is the best player I have at the position. A left-hander does have a few advantages, however, in fielding bunts, throwing to second base, starting the double play, tagging runners on pickoffs, and protecting the hole between first and second base.

The first baseman handles the ball as much as anyone on the field other than the catcher. He must give up the ball to the pitcher when the pitcher covers first base, start double plays, field bunts, catch fly balls, hold runners on base, tag them on pickoffs, be a cutoff man at times, receive balls from other infielders, participate in rundowns, and handle first-and-third situations. In this chapter we will discuss some of the first baseman's basic responsibilities. In the next chapter, we will look into his double-play and cutoff techniques.

Let's first discuss the first baseman's technique in receiving balls from the other infielders. As the ground ball is hit, the first baseman should hustle to the base, square his chest to the fielder, and prepare mentally for a difficult throw. His feet should be moving slightly as the infielder releases the ball (figure 9.1). The first baseman stretches toward the ball and, in most cases, his throwing-side foot tags the front edge of the base as he stretches toward the ball with his glove-side leg. To maximize the stretch, the first baseman must not extend his lead foot until he sees the path of the ball. He extends to the ball by bending his knees and extending his glove to shorten the distance of the throw (figure 9.2). If the throw is low, he should bend his knees as far as he can to keep his palm perpendicular to the ball and his elbow below the glove. Only on a very low throw should the first baseman turn the glove over and catch with his palm up.

One of the most difficult plays for the first baseman is receiving a throw from the catcher when the catcher is in front of home plate. This circumstance may occur when the batter bunts in front of the plate or when the catcher blocks a pitch in the dirt and must retrieve it from in front of the plate. The first baseman will need to tag the bag with his glove-side foot and square up his body to the ball (figure 9.3). By using this technique, he has a better chance to block the ball on a wild throw to first, thus preventing other runners on base from advancing.

Figure 9.1 The first baseman prepares to receive the throw from the infielder.

Figure 9.2 The first baseman bends his knees and extends his glove to the ball.

Figure 9.3 When preparing to receive a throw from the catcher, the first baseman tags the bag with his glove-side foot and squares his body to the ball.

Holding Runners on First. Another responsibility of the first baseman is holding runners on base. The outside of his right foot should touch first base with his left foot almost on the first-base line (figure 9.4a). His glove should be about thigh high, open, and ready for the pickoff throw. His feet should be about shoulder-width apart with his knees bent.

His first responsibility on a pickoff throw is to handle the tough throw. Upon receiving the throw, he slaps down a quick tag to the ground near the back corner of the base (figure 9.4b). He lets the ball do the traveling rather than reaching out to receive it.

a

b

Figure 9.4 Picking off a runner at first base. *(a)* The first baseman's right foot touches first base, his left foot is near the base line, his glove is open to the pitcher, ready to receive the pickoff throw. *(b)* The first baseman receives the pickoff throw and puts down the tag near the back corner of the base.

Executing When the Pitcher Covers First. Quite often, the first baseman fields a ground ball and must throw to the pitcher covering first base. The players should practice this fielding situation at least a few times each week. The first baseman should communicate ahead of time to the pitcher, reminding the pitcher of his responsibility to cover first base if the ball is hit to the first baseman. As the ball is hit, the first baseman fields the ball and calls to the pitcher that he has the ball. The first baseman starts to the bag with the ball and, if necessary, flips the ball underhand to the pitcher (figure 9.5). He should give the ball to the pitcher at chin level three steps before the pitcher reaches the bag.

An overhand throw is sometimes necessary, but an underhand throw is easier to execute and easier for the pitcher to see.

Fielding Bunts. Fielding bunts requires a great deal of communication and body control. Upon reading the bunt, the first baseman must decide whether to field the ball or cover the base and allow the pitcher to field it. When in doubt, he fields the ball, calls it loud and clear, and lets the pitcher or second baseman cover the bag. In our way of communicating, if the first baseman says anything at all it means that he will take the ball and that the pitcher or second baseman should cover the bag.

Fielding Fly Balls. Another important duty of a first baseman is fielding fly balls. Figure 9.6 delineates the area that is his responsibility. The first baseman should be aggressive, know the abilities of the fielders around him, and be aware of the extent of the foul-territory area. In most priority schemes for fly balls, the first baseman has the authority to call off the pitcher and catcher.

Second Baseman

Your second baseman should be an athletic player with quick feet, a strong arm, good agility, and excellent hands. Most of today's professional second basemen are former shortstops who moved to second base. Second basemen must be able to change direc-

Figure 9.5 The first baseman flips the ball underhand to the pitcher covering first.

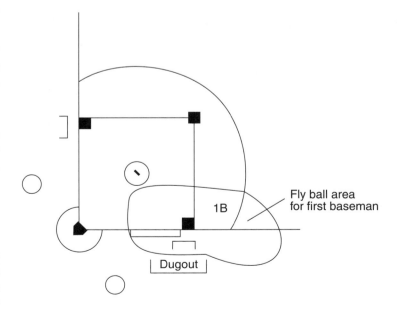

Figure 9.6 The zone for the first baseman fielding a fly ball.

tions, keep their balance when doing so, and throw accurately from all angles. Some of the responsibilities of the second baseman include positioning properly; fielding ground balls; starting and finishing double plays; handling pickoffs with the pitcher and catcher; executing rundowns, cutoffs, and relay situations; handling first-and-third defensive situations; tagging runners on steal attempts; and handling pop-ups in his area. We will discuss double plays and cutoff responsibilities in the next chapter. In this section we will talk about the second baseman's role on fly balls and tagging.

Fielding Fly Balls.   Your second baseman must be adept at fielding fly balls and ground balls. In most cases, second basemen (and all infielders in general) work more on ground balls than on fly balls. It is important that all infielders work on fly balls to understand their areas of responsibility and the communication involved.

The second baseman's job on fly balls is to be aggressive in his area. If he has any doubt, he should call off the first baseman and pitcher. He needs to be adept at going back on the ball, moving to his left and right, and coming in on the ball as well. Encourage the second baseman to field all the fly balls he can in pregame batting practice as well as in all practice sessions. Reserve time for setting up a Ponza machine at home plate to challenge your infielders on fly balls in their respective areas.

Tagging Runners.   All infielders need to be adept at tagging out runners. The fundamentals are similar for all infielders. We will outline the footwork and glove work of the second baseman fielding a throw from the catcher in a steal situation.

The second baseman arrives at the base early enough to set up and get his balance. He is ready to handle an off-target throw, if necessary. I encourage young players to set up in a position with their feet in front of second base at a 45-degree angle off the straight line from home plate to second base (figure 9.7). This positioning makes it easier for the second baseman to handle the throw up the line toward first base as well as the throw to his right side.

As the throw approaches the fielder, he replaces his left foot with his right foot, and his left foot straddles the base. The fielder allows the ball to travel and avoids reaching to catch it. He receives the ball deep in the glove over the front corner of the base.

As he receives the ball, he immediately slaps the tag down to the ground between the slider and the base (figure 9.8). After he tags the runner's foot or hand, he swipes the ball through the tag and spins out of the tag by pivoting on his right foot. He squares his shoulders and prepares to throw to the plate if necessary, as would be the case in a first-and-third situation (figure 9.9).

Figure 9.7   The second baseman setting up at second base with his feet in front of the base at a 45-degree angle to home plate.

Figure 9.8 The second baseman puts down the tag.

Figure 9.9 After tagging the runner, the second baseman pivots to throw home if necessary.

Shortstop

Your shortstop should have exceptional field awareness, leadership qualities, and athletic and improvisational ability. He should possess a thorough knowledge of the angles of the game, be able to throw at different angles, and have consistent hands. A shortstop who has consistent hands and feet, makes the routine plays, and has the ability to make the great play is a tremendous asset to any team. A strong, accurate arm allows him to play a little deeper and increases his range. Quick lateral movement, explosiveness, and great balance are qualities of great shortstops. Now playing in the major leagues are several outstanding shortstops, such as Nomar Garciaparra, Alex Rodriguez, and Derek Jeter. Rarely do you see a team win it all without an outstanding middle-infield combination.

A shortstop has many responsibilities. He should play in a position appropriate to the situation and within his own strengths and weaknesses. He must be able to field all types of ground balls, start and finish double plays, handle bunt situations, defend first-and-third situations, execute pickoffs and rundowns, recognize steal situations, execute cutoffs and relays, make tag plays, and handle fly balls.

One of the shortstop's most important responsibilities is to be a team and defensive leader. His alertness can inspire the rest of the team. Because he is in the middle of the action, he must have outstanding anticipation and communication skills.

Third Baseman

Your third baseman needs to be an aggressive, tough player. His ability to handle the slow-roller play and bunt situations is critical. His first step is important because batted balls get to him very quickly. A strong accurate arm will allow him to make a wider variety of plays. As with the other infielders, his ability and the game situation determine his positioning.

The third baseman must be adept at fielding bunts and handling bunt situations. Our communication system is built around the idea of the third baseman being aggressive. He must call off the pitcher on bunts if there is any question about which of them should field the ball. His first priority should be to cover the ball; covering third base is his second priority. The catchy phrase we use is "When in doubt, get the out!" This simply means that if the third baseman has any question in his mind about whether to field the ball or retreat to cover the base, he is aggressive and uses his fielding strengths and better angle to field the ball and secure the out.

OUTFIELDERS

The outfielders must work together as a group by communicating aggressively with each other. Anticipation and concentration skills are important as are speed, agility, and throwing ability. The outfielders must take pride in not allowing any fly balls to hit the ground. The center fielder has fly-ball priority over both the left fielder and right fielder and should be the leader in communicating and positioning.

Left and Right Fielders

The two corner outfielders must be able to judge spin on fly balls, bat angles, and points of contact with the bat and ball. Their feet must be able to move and adjust quickly to the spin and change of direction of the ball as it heads into their areas of responsibility. A high concentration level and knowledge of the angles of the game are essential to the success of a left or right fielder. In most cases, you would rather have the stronger arm in right field than left field because the right fielder must make longer throws to third base. We talked about fielding fly balls in a previous chapter, but it is important to talk about fielding ground balls from an outfielder's viewpoint.

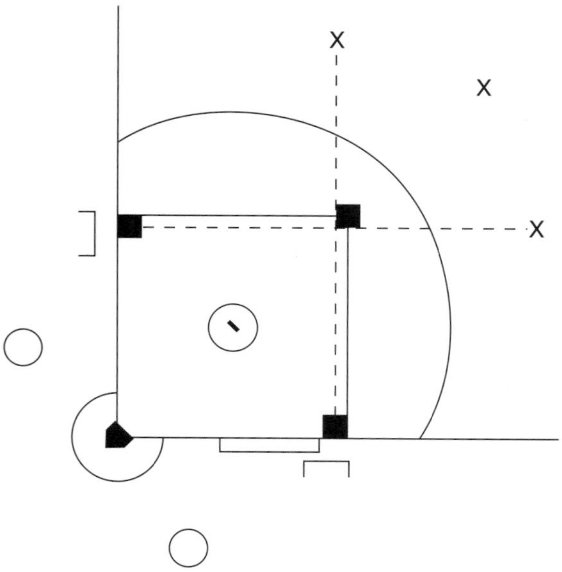

Positioning. Again, positioning is determined by the hitter, the pitch being thrown, the location of the pitch, the bat angle of the swing, the wind conditions, the size of the field, the game situation, the type of hitter, and the player's strengths and weaknesses.

Young players seem to have difficulty finding a starting point in their positioning. I usually tell the right fielder to start at a position that would be in a straight line from third base through second base and then move from there according to the factors mentioned earlier. The left fielder could start at a position that would be a straight line from first base through second base (figure 9.10).

Figure 9.10 Positioning for right and left fielders, before taking into consideration the other factors.

Fielding Ground Balls. Players should field ground balls to the outfield with these considerations in mind:

- Is there an immediate play to be made and a throw to be executed?
- How hard was the ball hit?
- Am I being backed up by my next closest outfielder?
- What type of surface am I on, and how smooth is the approach of the ball?
- What are my abilities?

Figure 9.11 shows the technique the outfielder should use on a ball hit hard right at him, on a rough surface, with no immediate need to throw. The throwing-hand knee drops to the ground, the shoulders stay square to the ball, and the glove hand and throwing hand drop to the space between the legs and remain open to the ball. The glove-hand leg is out to the side with the foot positioned at about a 45-degree angle to the ball.

Figure 9.12 shows the infield method of fielding a ground ball. The outfielder uses this technique when he may need

Figure 9.11 Hard ground ball fielded by an outfielder on a rough surface with no immediate throw needed.

Figure 9.12 The infield method used by an outfielder when he must throw immediately. (a) The outfielder squares his body, hands in front, and fields the ball off his glove-hand eye. (b) The outfielder secures the ball before starting the crow hop.

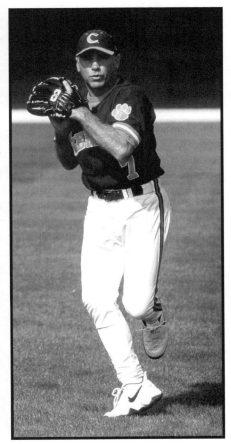

a   b

Figure 9.13 The outfielder fields the ball with his glove hand alone when the game is on the line.

to throw immediately and when he is on a smoother surface. The outfielder fields the ball like an infielder by squaring his body, keeping his hands in front, fielding off the glove-hand eye, and securing the ball back into the center of his body before kicking through in front to start the crow hop.

The third method is called the glove-hand-alone method or do-or-die method. The outfielder uses this technique so that he can make an immediate play when the game is on the line (figure 9.13). He approaches the ball aggressively and, as the ball nears, shuffles his feet to steady himself and gain balance. He extends his glove low and toward the ball just off to the side of his glove-side foot. He fields the ball with his knees bent and his head locked on the ball. The glove and ball start to travel up to the throwing position as he begins to crow hop.

Center Fielder

The center fielder will dictate, in many ways, the defensive success of your team. He needs to be athletic, quick, fast, and aggressive. He controls the defensive positioning of the outfield and has fly-ball priority over any other player on the field. An aggressive center fielder can cover both gaps, allowing you to place in left or right field a strong hitter who may not have outstanding defensive ability and speed. A team should be strong up the middle, and your center fielder is a great place to start building your team.

Your center fielder needs to talk to and position the other outfielders. His positioning is dictated by his abilities as well as the abilities of the other outfielders. Because of his position on the field, he has the highest fly-ball priority. Everyone should give way if he calls the ball.

Teams with a Willie Mays or Ken Griffey Jr. in center field have a tremendous advantage. A strong center fielder creates the impression that an out will be recorded on every fly ball hit to the outfield. When building a team, start with a strong center fielder, shortstop, and catcher.

Executing Double Plays and Relays

In this chapter, we will discuss double plays and cutoff and relay situations. The team that can execute these plays is usually well coached and extremely tough to beat.

DOUBLE PLAYS

The double play is one of the more exciting plays in baseball. Teams that can consistently execute it are usually championship-caliber teams. The double play is the pitcher's best friend—with one pitch he can record two outs and get out of a jam. The momentum of the game often changes on a double play.

All strong defensive teams have athletes up the middle who can turn the double play. Execution requires a series of skills that your team should practice daily in workouts. Double plays can occur in a variety of ways. Your team should practice making the play at all angles on many different types of ground balls.

In this chapter, we will focus on starting the double play from the shortstop, second-base, first-base, and third-base positions and finishing it from the perspective of the shortstop and second baseman.

6-4-3 Double Play

This double-play ball is usually hit toward the second-base bag, hit hard directly at the shortstop, or hit hard a little to his left or right. The shortstop should attack the ball and make fielding contact with it as quickly as he can. With each bounce, the runner closes in on first base. Most double plays must be turned within 4.0 to 4.5 seconds from the time the ball is hit. We use the phrase "You be sure, he'll be quick" to emphasize that the player starting the double play must be accurate with his feed to get the play started. The only way the defense can turn the double play is for the starter to get to the ball quickly and then make an accurate feed.

Let's talk first about the basic double-play starts a shortstop must be able to make. On a ball hit right at him, the shortstop uses a body-foot pivot to start the double play if an underhand feed is not appropriate. As the shortstop readies himself to field the ground ball, he drop steps slightly with his left foot to open up more to the second baseman. He fields the ball with good mechanics—out in front, in the center of his body, and with his knees bent. He brings the ball into the belt area and moves it quickly to a short-throw position with his arm about parallel to the ground (figure 10.1). As he becomes more proficient and confident, he can release the ball from closer to where he fielded the ball. His feet, knees, and belt buckle should be pointing toward his target when he throws. He should direct the throw to the closest corner of second base about chest high.

On a ground ball taking him toward second base, the shortstop fields the ball with two hands and has his knees bent. After fielding the ball, he separates his hands, brings his glove toward his left shoulder, and provides a stiff-wristed underhand toss to the second baseman (figure 10.2). He follows his toss with the nose-to-leather idea.

Occasionally the shortstop must move to his backhand side to field the ball and start the double play. As he attacks the ball to his right, he steps around it with his right foot, opens his left foot to the second baseman, stays low, and gets rid of the ball quickly and firmly. Time is critical on this type of ground ball.

Figure 10.1 The shortstop in the short-throw position.

Figure 10.2 The shortstop uses a stiff-wristed underhand toss to the second baseman.

5-4-3 Double Play

Although the third baseman will have opportunities to start the double play from different positions and depths, the principles for all plays are basically the same. The ball normally gets to the third baseman a little more quickly than it does to the shortstop, but he must field it cleanly and make an accurate feed to the second baseman. He should approach the ball by getting around it slightly, creating an angle, and opening up slightly with his left foot. He looks the ball into the body and then releases a strong, accurate throw either from the glove area or from a higher arm angle depending on how quickly the ball reached him and how quick the runner is. Depending on how strong his arm is, he can either throw the ball to second base with no steps or replace the left foot with the right foot to strengthen his throw and improve his accuracy.

The third baseman will at times have to start a double play by backhanding the ball. On a ball that takes him toward second base, he will have to throw on the run. At any rate, his throws should be chest high over the inside corner of second base.

4-6-3 Double Play

The second baseman can start the double play in a variety of ways. We are going to talk about three basic angles and the options he has from these areas. In a double-play situation, the second baseman will normally be playing a step closer in and a step closer to the base.

Figure 10.3 The second baseman uses a stiff-wristed underhand toss to get the ball to the shortstop.

If a ball is hit toward second base, the second baseman should position his body in front of the baseball, bend his knees, field the ball on the right side of his body with two hands, and look the ball into the glove. After fielding the ball, he starts to break his hands and delivers the ball to the shortstop chest high on the inside corner of second base, with a stiff-wristed underhand toss (figure 10.3). He follows his throw by looking it into the shortstop's glove.

A stiff-wristed backhand toss can be used by the advanced player (figure 10.4). I prefer the underhand toss because it seems more accurate for the young player and the shortstop can see the ball better in most cases.

If the ball is hit at the second baseman and he is too far away to underhand or backhand toss to the shortstop, he has a couple of options depending on his arm strength. The most accurate and quickest way is to use the body-foot pivot (figure 10.5). Here the second baseman drop steps slightly with his right foot, fields the ball off the center of his body, and pivots his feet, knees, and belt buckle to the shortstop. After fielding the ball, the fielder brings the ball to the center of his body and then throws it with his forearm angled about 45 degrees to the ground.

If the ball is hit to the second baseman's left, he can use the jump pivot, which requires him to jump, turn, and replace his feet after fielding the ball. After jump pivoting,

Figure 10.4 An advanced player can use the stiff-wristed backhand toss.

Figure 10.5 The body-foot pivot.

the player must be sure to line up his feet and shoulders to second base. He must also stay low and not raise his center of gravity.

A ball hit far to the second baseman's glove side requires some judgment. Even if he must field the ball one handed and outside his feet, he may have a chance to get the lead runner if the ground ball has traveled in front of the runner. If the ground ball travels behind the runner, the second baseman should throw to first base for the sure out. If the second baseman decides he has a chance at the lead runner, he will field the ball with one hand, reverse pivot with his back to the infield, and line up his feet and shoulders to second base before throwing to the shortstop.

3-6-3 Double Play

The first baseman can start this double play from either of two positions—from the position he uses to hold the runner on first base or from a deeper position behind the runner.

A left-handed first baseman will mirror the technique of the third baseman in starting the double play. He will secure the ball and then either replace his feet with momentum toward the shortstop or throw with no steps if he has a strong arm. Occasionally he will have to retreat to the base after throwing the ball to finish the double play. At times, the pitcher takes over the job of finishing the double play by covering first base. The first baseman and pitcher must practice this play a great deal and must communicate so that both do not end up at first base.

A right-handed first baseman has some other things to consider when starting the double play. On the ball hit at him, whether he is playing in front of the bag or behind it, he jump pivots and delivers a strong, accurate throw to either the inside or outside of second base depending on where he fields the ball.

On a ball hit to his backhand side, the first baseman just steps through with his right foot and delivers the throw to the shortstop.

On a hard-hit ball to his forehand side that he must field one handed outside his feet, he can reverse pivot just as the second baseman does on the same ball.

Finishing the Double Play

The player finishing the double play can use any of several methods, but some key principles apply to most situations:

- The player should always expect the tough throw and be prepared to handle it.
- He must be sure to get one out before trying for the second.
- "Know when to hold them, know when to fold them." If there is no chance to get the second out, the fielder should not throw the ball to try creating a play that is not there.
- The player should try to catch the ball with balance and with momentum headed toward first base.
- He should not move toward first base until he sees the ball coming to him accurately.
- The fielder should try to catch the ball inside his feet with both hands off the left chest.

Second Baseman Finishing the Double Play. The second baseman can turn the double play in several ways. As a coach you will have to determine which footwork is most comfortable for your second baseman. No one technique works for every player.

Young players who need help with their arms may find the following technique the most effective. The young second baseman gets to the bag quickly and sets with his feet positioned behind second base, his chest and feet parallel to the third-base line, and his weight on the balls of his feet. His hands are positioned and ready for the ball at chest level with thumbs up and to the inside, prepared for the tough throw (figure 10.6a).

This positioning helps on a poor feed to the back side of the base because the second baseman is already there and can catch the ball inside his feet and on balance. He can then step on the bag with his left foot as he throws to first base to complete the double play.

When the ball is delivered perfectly over the inside corner of the base, the young second baseman replaces his left foot with his right and then straddles the base with his left foot (figure 10.6b). He catches the ball with two hands off his left chest as the left foot nears the ground. His momentum is now headed toward first base, and he should be able to throw harder and more accurately to first. As he receives the ball, his hands stay above the chest to save time. The arc of his throw is quick, and his arm should be parallel to the ground or higher when delivering the ball to first.

a

b

Figure 10.6 A young second baseman finishes a double play by (a) getting ready to receive the ball by positioning his feet behind the base and (b) straddling the base as he receives the ball.

Teach your young second baseman that once he releases the ball to first, he should get in the air to avoid the slide and keep his feet off the ground in case the runner makes contact.

A more advanced, stronger player can position himself near the closer back corner (figure 10.7) of second base. As he receives an accurate feed, he steps to the ball with his right foot, still catching the ball off the left side of the chest. His knees are bent as he receives the ball, and he keeps his hands above chest level. The second baseman transfers the ball to his throwing hand and releases it as he steps with his left foot. Fewer steps are required, and the advanced player has enough arm strength to finish the play.

On a ground ball that brings the shortstop very close to the bag, the second baseman will sometimes choose to stay on his side of the base, touch second base with his left foot (figure 10.8), receive the throw, rock back, and then step toward first base to finish the double play.

If the second baseman receives the ball too early on his way to the bag, he must improvise to hit the bag with his right foot and immediately throw to first base.

Shortstop Finishing the Double Play. The shortstop must move to his position quickly and prepare for the toughest possible throw. He should move his feet behind second base, with his shoulders nearly square to the first-base line (figure 10.9). He should be ready to receive the ball with two hands as he steps into the ball with his left foot.

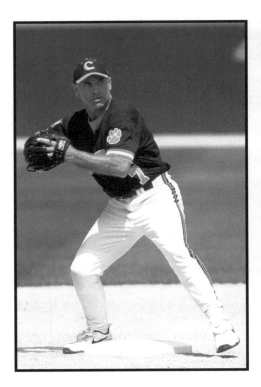

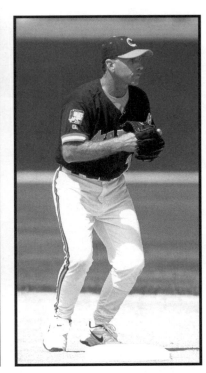

Figure 10.7 An advanced second baseman positions himself near the closer back corner of the bag.

Figure 10.8 The second baseman stays on his side of the base, touching the base with his left foot.

Figure 10.9 The shortstop moves his feet behind second base and squares his shoulders to the base line.

After receiving the ball, he drags his right foot across the bag in front of his left foot. He transfers the ball to his throwing hand by keeping his hands chest level or above if possible and delivers a strong throw to first with his arm parallel to the ground or higher. After releasing the ball, he jumps slightly into the air to avoid a collision at second base.

If the throw is being delivered on the infield side by the first baseman, the short-stop sets up on the inside of second base. The shortstop has his left foot on the base when he receives the throw. He kicks in front with his right foot and then with his left foot to throw.

CUTOFFS AND RELAYS

To prevent the opposition from taking extra bases and to avoid big innings, a team must be able to handle cutoff and relay situations efficiently. Several basic principles govern the cutoff scheme:

- Fielders generally throw the ball one base ahead of the lead runner.
- Every man has a job to do on every play.
- The throw to the cutoff man should hit him chest to head high.
- Fielders must think about what they may have to do with the ball before it comes to them.
- Players should communicate confidently and loudly with teammates.
- All calls should be loud and repetitive.

To learn to handle the ball and relay it properly, we first need to look at the technique of the cutoff and relay men.

Figure 10.10 The relay man in position to receive the throw.

Cutoff and Relay Technique

First, the ball handlers must always position themselves in the way they expect to handle the ball, positions that allows them to make strong, accurate throws. The cutoff and relay men should be in position to make a perfect throw to the intended base if needed. They should never position themselves farther from the target than their abilities allow.

The relay man should have his hands in the air to give a target to the outfielder (figure 10.10). His feet should be moving slightly to help him adjust to the ball. As the ball is released in his direction, the relay man should work hard to keep the ball on his glove side and turn to the side so that he receives the ball almost in front of his face. As he catches the ball, he turns his head to the target and with a right-left step (for a right-handed thrower) throws to the base. His hands should not drop below his chest because he must throw the ball quickly.

Cutoff and Relay Situations

Your team needs to know how to handle seven basic situations:

1. No one on base, single to left field, center field, or right field.
2. Man on first, single to left field, center field, or right field.
3. Man on second, single to left field, center field, or right field.
4. Men on first and second, single to left field, center field, or right field.
5. No one on base, extra-base hit.
6. Man on first, extra-base hit.
7. Man on third, fly ball to left field, center field, or right field.

In regular cutoff situations we use the label 1 for first base, 2 for second base, 3 for third base, and 4 for home plate. The first call man, always the outfielder closest to the one making the play, calls the base that the fielder should throw to. The second call man lines up the cutoff man in a straight line to the intended base and then calls the base number, indicating where the ball should be relayed. If the second call man yells "Cut," the relay man looks for a back-side play or runs the ball back to the infield. If the second call man makes no sound at all, he wants the ball to travel through without being cut off. He can then decoy the runner and hope to make a tag for the out. He will do this only if the throw is on line and if he will be able to field the throw cleanly.

Strong, confident communication is necessary. Players must make decisions based on the likelihood of tagging the runner out and not allowing other runners to advance to better scoring positions.

Now let's look at each of the seven basic situations.

No One on Base, Single to Left Field, Center Field, or Right Field.   On a single hit to left field with the bases empty, the left fielder fields the ball, the center fielder becomes the first call man, the shortstop becomes the cutoff man, and the second baseman is the second call man (figure 10.11a). The center fielder calls to the left fielder to throw to second base. After hearing the call from the center fielder, the left fielder throws the ball through the shortstop to second base. The second baseman lines up the shortstop and then either tells him to cut off the ball or says nothing to indicate that he wants the ball to come through.

When the bases are empty and a single is hit to center field, the outfielder closest to the center fielder becomes the first call man (in figure 10.11b, the right fielder is closer). He calls for the center fielder to throw the ball to second base. The cutoff man is either the second baseman or the shortstop, whichever one is closer to the fielded ball; the other middle infielder becomes the second call man. The second call man lines up the cutoff man and makes the call on whether the ball should be cut off or allowed to come through.

When the bases are empty and a single is hit to right field, the center fielder hustles over to help the right fielder and makes the call to throw to second base. The shortstop, who becomes the second call man, lines up the second baseman and then makes the call on whether the ball should be cut off (figure 10.11c).

Man on First, Single to Left Field, Center Field, or Right Field.   In all three of these situations, the outfielder closer to the player fielding the ball makes the call

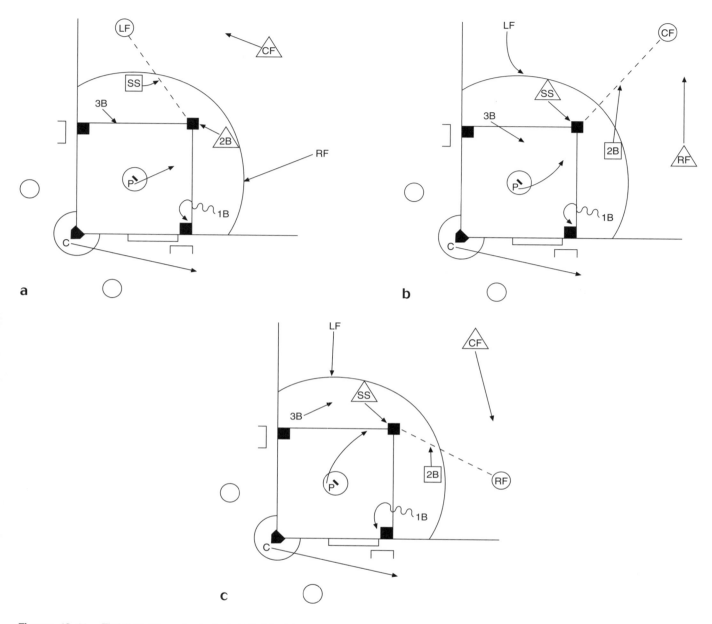

Figure 10.11 Fielding (a) a single to left field with no runners on base, (b) a single to center field with no runners on base, and (c) a single to right field with no runners on base.

to throw toward third base. The shortstop is the cutoff man, and the third baseman lines him up. The third baseman then makes the call on whether the ball should be cut off or allowed to travel through to third base (figure 10.12).

Man on Second, Single to Left Field, Center Field, or Right Field. On a single to left field with a runner on second, the center fielder makes the initial call for the left fielder to throw the ball to home plate. The third baseman is the cutoff man. The catcher lines up the third baseman in a straight line to home plate. The catcher calls whether the throw should be cut off or allowed to go through to home plate (figure 10.13a).

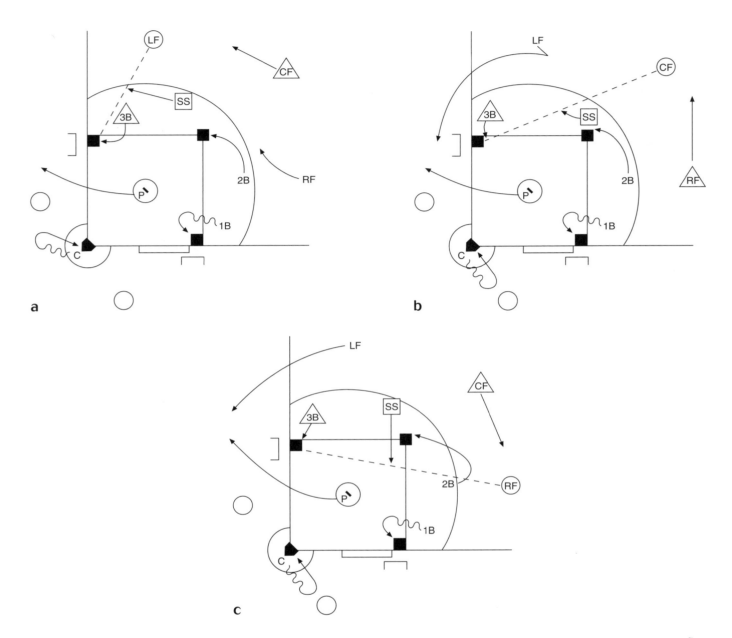

Figure 10.12 Fielding (a) a single to left field with a runner on first base, (b) a single to center field with a runner on first base, and (c) a single to right field with a runner on first base.

On a single to center field or right field with a runner on second, the outfielder closer to the player fielding the ball makes the initial call to throw to home plate. The first baseman is the cutoff man. The catcher lines up the first baseman and then makes the call on whether the throw should be cut off or allowed to go through home plate (figures 10.13b and 10.13c).

Men on First and Second, Single to Left Field, Center Field, or Right Field. In this situation the outfielder has three options on where to throw the ball—home plate (to get the lead runner), third base, or second base. The first two options, the best options, are shown in figure 10.14.

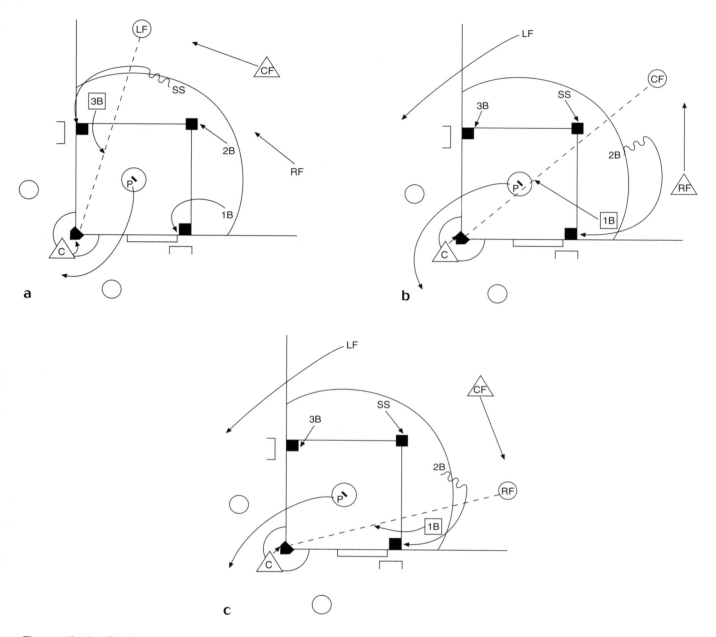

Figure 10.13 Fielding (a) a single to left field with a runner on second base, (b) a single to center field with a runner on second base, and (c) a single to right field with a runner on second base.

The first option would be to throw to home plate to get the lead runner. On a single to left field, the initial call to throw home comes from the center fielder. The third baseman lines up as the cutoff man, and the catcher becomes the second call man (figure 10.14a). The catcher either calls for the ball to be cut off and thrown to another base or says nothing so that it comes to home plate. On a single to center field or right field, the initial call to throw home comes from the closer outfielder (in figure 10.14b, the right fielder; in figure 10.14c, the center fielder). The catcher lines up the first baseman, who is the cutoff man, and either calls for the ball to be cut off or says nothing so that the ball comes through.

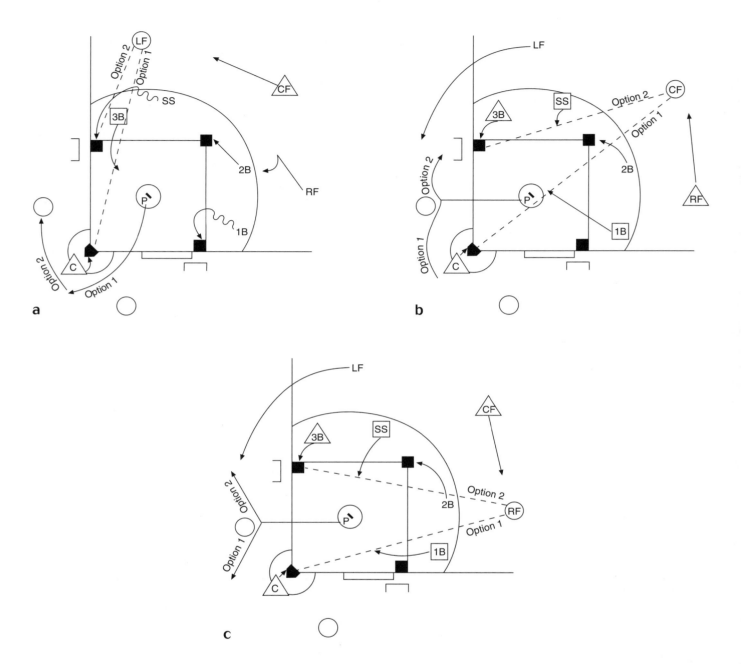

Figure 10.14 Fielding (a) a single to left field with runners on first and second base, (b) a single to center field with runners on first and second base, and (c) a single to right field with runners on first and second base.

In the second option, the first call man (the closer outfielder) calls for the throw to go to third base. On a single to left field, this would be a direct throw from the left fielder to the shortstop covering third base. On a single to center field or right field, the throw goes through the shortstop toward third base. The third baseman is the second call man and makes the call on whether the ball should be cut off or allowed to go through to third base.

Only when there is no chance to record an out at home plate or third base should the throw go to second base to keep the batter from moving into a better scoring position. This throw would go directly from the fielder to the second baseman. The closer outfielder would make the call.

No One on Base, Extra-Base Hit.   When the bases are empty and the batter gets an extra-base hit, the goal is to hold the batter to as few extra bases as possible. As the outfielder fields the ball at or near the fence, the closer outfielder makes the call to the fielder on where to throw the ball. In this situation, the call is usually to throw to third base (figure 10.15). The middle infielders line up in what is called a double relay. The middle infielder closer to the ball moves to the relay position. The other middle infielder is the call man. He takes a position 15 feet behind the relay man and lines him up. The trail infielder is in position to field an overthrown ball from the outfielder or an underthrown ball on the long hop. The first baseman trails the runner to second base to prevent a large turn by the runner.

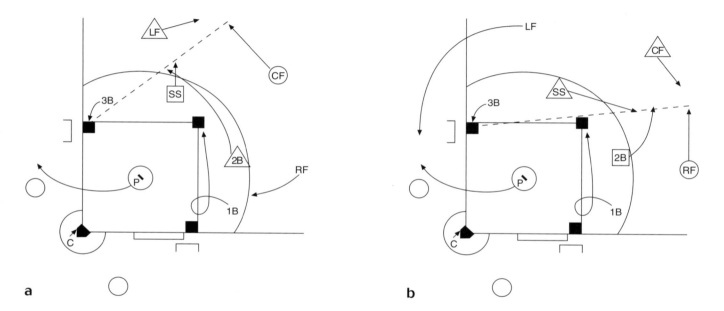

Figure 10.15   Fielding (a) an extra-base hit to left-center field with no runners on base and (b) an extra-base hit to right-center field with no runners on base.

Man on First, Extra-Base Hit.   The execution of this situation is similar to the execution used for an extra-base hit with no one on base. The difference is that the outfielder throws to the double relay toward home plate rather than third base and the infielders line up to home plate. The catcher then lines up the first baseman behind the trailing infielder and either calls for the first baseman to cut off the throw to the plate and redirect it to another base or says nothing and allows it to come through to him (figure 10.16a).

On an extra-base hit to right-center field, the defense also has the option to throw to third base to get the lead runner. The second call man, the shortstop, makes this call to the second baseman, who turns and throws to third after catching the throw from the center fielder (figure 10.16b).

Man on Third, Fly Ball to Left Field, Center Field, or Right Field.   On a fly ball to left field with a runner on third, the third baseman is the cutoff man on the throw to

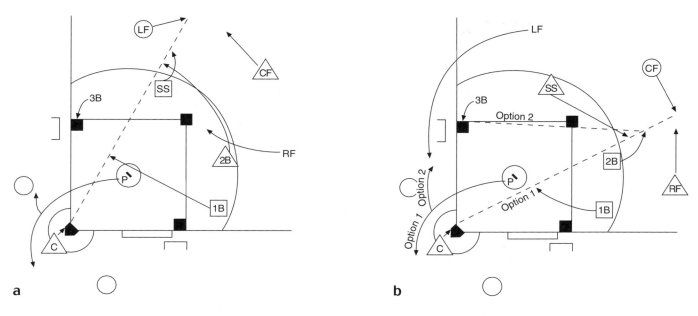

Figure 10.16   Fielding (a) an extra-base hit to left-center field with a runner on first base and (b) an extra-base hit to right-center field with a runner on first base.

home plate. The catcher lines him up and makes the call whether the ball should be cut off or not (figure 10.17a).

On a fly ball to center field or right field with a runner on third, the first baseman becomes the cutoff man. The catcher lines him up and makes the call on whether the throw should be cut off or not. Figure 10.17b shows how the defense would play a fly ball to right field.

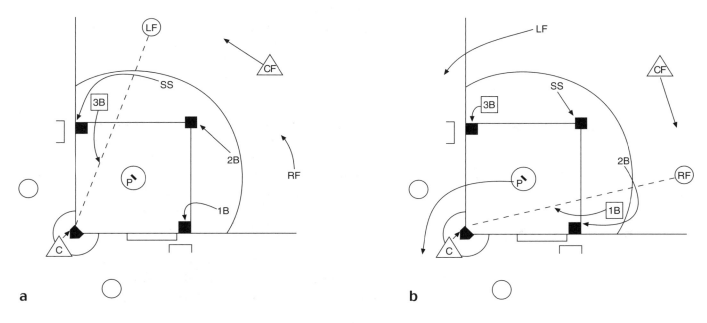

Figure 10.17   Fielding (a) a fly ball to left field with a runner on third base and (b) a fly ball to right field with a runner on third base.

Double Relays

Double relays are used on extra-base hits that take an outfielder to the fence. The goal is to get the ball in quickly enough to hold the hitter to a double.

As the ball heads to the fence, the closer middle infielder becomes the relay man. He positions himself in a straight line between the ball and the intended base (third or home). The trailing infielder takes a position 15 feet behind the relay man. He is there to call where the throw should be made and to handle an overthrown or underthrown ball. The first relay man should let the ball go to the second infielder if he has to leave his feet to catch it or if the ball is going to hit the ground and short hop him. The relay men should learn to go out no farther than the spot from which they can throw a strike to the proper base.

DOUBLE-PLAY DRILLS

Short-Distance Double-Play Drill

Purpose: To provide many repetitions at a short distance in a controlled atmosphere, practicing all double-play starts and finishes.

Procedure:

1. The shortstops and second basemen line up in their respective positions. A first baseman stands at first to complete the double play. The coach kneels 10 to 15 yards in front of the shortstops with a bucket of balls (figure 10.18).

2. The coach rolls one ball after another to the shortstop, simulating the starts of different types of double plays.

3. The shortstop uses the proper technique to start the double play. He throws the ball to the second baseman, who continues the double-play execution to the first baseman 45 feet away.

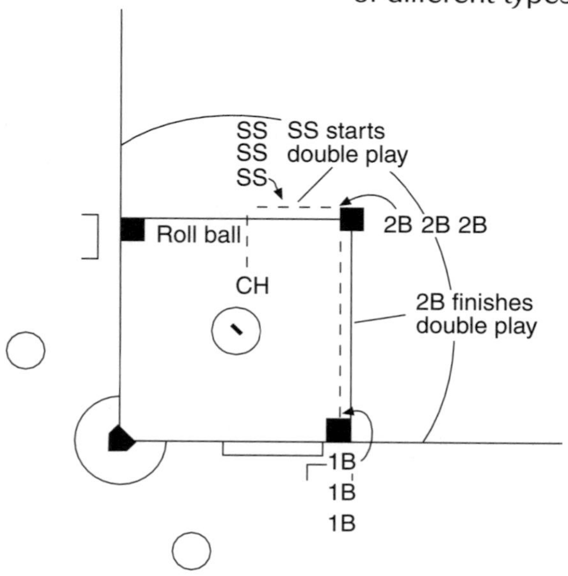

Coaching Points: The coach rolls balls continuously to the shortstops, starting the double play for many controlled repetitions. He should emphasize fundamentals and proper technique for starting the double play. The coach can then create different ground balls and angles for starting double plays from both the shortstop and second-base positions. He should also stress proper fundamentals for finishing the double play.

Figure 10.18 Setup for the Short-Distance Double-Play drill.

Live Double Plays During Batting Practice

Purpose: To encourage infielders to turn double plays from all angles from live balls hit during batting practice.

Procedure:

1. During batting practice, one full infield unit gets into position.
2. Each ground ball hit is a double-play situation and is executed quickly at game speed.

Coaching Points: Require infielders to attack the ball off the bat and turn over the double play in 4.3 seconds or less. This drill allows all infielders to practice starting and finishing the double play in gamelike conditions.

CUTOFF AND RELAY DRILLS

Relay Technique and Ball-Handling Drill

Purpose: To learn how to handle relay throws and work on proper technique in executing relays.

Procedure:

1. Three infielders stand in a straight line approximately 120 feet apart. The middle infielder is in proper relay position (figure 10.19).
2. The middle infielder receives the ball from the end infielder. He uses proper relay-handling technique to throw the ball to the other end infielder, who in turn tags an imaginary base runner, spins, and throws back to the middle infielder.
3. The middle infielder receives the relay throw and throws to the other end infielder, who tags the imaginary base runner, spins, and throws back to the middle infielder.

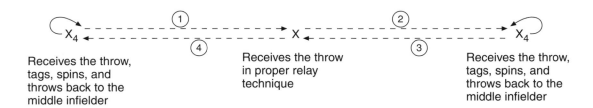

Figure 10.19 Setup for Relay Technique and Ball-Handling drill.

Coaching Points: The relay man in the middle should move his feet so that he is always ready for the next throw. He should turn his body to his glove side when receiving the throw. This drill focuses on proper relay technique but also provides an opportunity to work on tagging technique.

Cutoffs and Relays During Batting Practice

Purpose: To provide live repetitions in cutoff and relay situations during batting practice.

Procedure:

1. During batting practice, the infielders and outfielders play the ball live off the bat, working on their jumps, angles, and reads. The coach blows a whistle and signals to the outfielders the base that the next relay throw should go to.

2. On the next ball hit to the outfield, the outfielders and infielders execute the proper cutoff and relay situation based on the coach's instructions.

3. The batting-practice pitcher waits until the relay play is finished before throwing another pitch. Once the play is executed, batting practice continues.

4. The coach blows the whistle again to signal the next base that he wants the relay to go to.

Coaching Points: After they have received the signal from the coach, the fielders must stay alert and communicate with each other to complete the relay play successfully. The coach should emphasize to the outfielders that they must be aggressive in going to the ball and must make accurate throws. Infielders must take the proper cutoff and relay positions and use correct technique in finishing the play. Communication should be loud and clear.

PART III

Pitching and Catching

Although the techniques and responsibilities of pitchers and catchers contrast sharply, their roles on the team are tightly linked. A quality catcher can make an average pitching staff successful. Quality pitching can make up for errors in the field or a sluggish offense.

At Mississippi State, we teach our pitchers the Big 5 of pitching:

1. Pitch with a located fastball.
2. Develop a quick breaking ball.
3. Learn to change speeds.
4. Learn to pick off and hold runners.
5. Learn to field the position.

Implementing the phases of the Big 5 is discussed in detail in chapter 11, along with delivery mechanics and pitching technique and drills that emphasize the skills without overworking the arm. Chapter 12 contains information on throwing the quick breaking ball (phase 2) and changing speeds (phase 3), and chapter 13 covers locating the pitch (phase 1). Picking off and holding runners (phase 4) is covered in chapter 14, and fielding the pitcher's position (phase 5) is covered in chapter 15.

With hard work and consistent repetitions, pitchers can be successful. A solid delivery from the windup and stretch is critical; bullpen sessions and delivery drills are important teachers. The pitcher's knowledge of why his delivery is important gives him a kinesthetic awareness of his delivery. The pitcher grasps the feel of the delivery so that he can repeat it consistently. A location sequence for each pitch improves control and movement and gives the pitcher confidence to throw the ball through the strike zone.

A good pitcher understands three things. First, he isn't afraid of being hit. He understands the batters usually make outs when they hit the ball into fair territory. Second, he knows that he has a better chance of success against all hitters when he pitches ahead in the count. Statistics prove this every season. Third, he uses what he can do well and stays away from what he doesn't do well. Our simplified pitching rules give the pitcher the confidence to get hitters out using his strengths and avoiding low matchup percentages and his weaknesses.

Many other elements are essential to successful pitching—warm-up routines for starters and relievers, weight training, conditioning, care of the arm, proper stretching and rehabilitation, and mental concepts and mental training. The will to compete and live it all on the field is the exciting part of competition.

Catchers are leaders. A good catcher loves to wear his gear and is proud that he is the team's catcher. You can identify a good catcher by observing how he works with the pitchers in the bullpen. The way he handles himself and the way he earns the respect of the pitching staff and coaches says much about his dedication. A good catcher can make an average pitching staff much better, but the opposite is true as well. When a pitcher is afraid to throw a breaking ball in the dirt with two strikes or with runners on base, negative things usually happen. Good catchers have the will and ability to prevent pitches from getting past them.

Chapters 16 and 17 cover what it takes to develop a good catcher. Chapter 16 covers basic techniques and fundamentals for catching pitches, and chapter 17 discusses how catchers field plays.

11

Pitching Technique

Our pitching plan consists of five specific areas that we refer to as the Big 5. In essence, these areas define our pitchers' daily, weekly, monthly, and yearly practice plan. We individualize it in one-on-one teaching sessions so that the core plan remains in place. The Big 5 are the following:

1. Pitch with a located fastball.
2. Develop a quick breaking ball.
3. Learn to change speeds.
4. Learn to pick off and hold runners.
5. Learn to field the position.

Our pitchers accomplish phases 1, 2, and 3 by participating in delivery drills, working out in the bullpen, pitching batting practice, and pitching in scrimmage games. Pitchers work on phase 4 during our daily warm-up sessions with the Two-Line Pickoff drill, our Triangle Picks drill, and our Pickoff Drill Series With Position Players. Pitchers work on fielding plays (phase 5) during Pitcher's Pepper, during fielding practice on the field, or when our pitchers participate in the drill series with our position players.

We challenge our pitchers to do three things each time they pick up a baseball:

1. locate,
2. change speeds, and
3. pitch the ball with a sound mechanical delivery.

We will discuss changing speeds and locating pitches in the following chapters. In this chapter, we will focus on developing sound pitching technique and a good, solid delivery.

SOUND DELIVERY MECHANICS

Proper delivery mechanics enable a pitcher to do the following:

1. Generate optimal hand speed through the release point (velocity)
2. Impart maximum spin (fastball movement and tighter spin for breaking balls)
3. Keep the arm and body coordinated to release the ball consistently (control)
4. Reduce the likelihood of injury
5. Increase confidence

Our pitchers must work from both the full windup position and the stretch position to develop a sound delivery. During a game, pitchers generally use the windup position when the bases are empty. With a runner on base, pitchers use the stretch position so that the runner cannot take as big a lead and the pitcher can use his pickoff move to deter the runner. With a runner on third base or with the bases loaded, the pitcher can use either position. (I prefer the stretch position in that situation to keep leadoffs to a minimum.) Today you see many relief pitchers pitch only from the stretch position. The coach or the pitcher can make this choice.

The pitcher should use a simple delivery to enhance his chances of throwing each pitch consistently. Body control and balance throughout the delivery are important. Pitchers who can consistently repeat their deliveries locate the pitch better, pitch to advantage counts, and put their defense in position to make plays. Couple a consistent pitcher with a solid defense that loves to compete and you have the makings of a good pitcher.

The pitcher must be able to pitch to advantage counts. Year after year, statistics show that the batter behind in the count hits for a much lower batting average. We need to take advantage of the averages by throwing the ball into the strike zone early in the count. Our goal is to have the batter hit the ball in fair territory before the pitcher throws three pitches.

We break the delivery into five phases (see figure 11.1):

a

b

c

d

e

Figure 11.1 The delivery: *(a)* initial stance; *(b)* primary balance point; *(c)* break phase; *(d)* secondary power position; *(e)* follow-through.

1. the initial stance or setup,
2. the primary balance point,
3. the break phase,
4. the secondary power position, and
5. the follow-through.

To simplify discussion of the delivery, I will address only the major points. Remember that the delivery is a flowing action from one phase to another. Rhythm and tempo are important. The pitcher does not stop between phases, but for the benefit of teaching we distinguish five phases.

Initial Stance or Setup

The catcher uses the fingers of his throwing hand to indicate the pitch. He then moves his hand to indicate the location. The pitcher receives the pitch and location from the catcher and then prepares to pitch.

An important component at this stage is mental preparation. We use Dr. Bill Harrison's steps and add our own meaning:

1. Analyze—decide what pitch to throw and where to locate it.
2. Visualize—mentally see the pitch happening.
3. Centralize—breathe and focus on the pitch.
4. Execute—let it happen.

Figure 11.2 The initial stance for a right-handed pitcher.

For his initial stance (figure 11.2), the pitcher stands upright and relaxed. We like our right-handed pitchers to be on the right side of the pitching rubber and our left-handed pitchers to be on the left side. This positioning creates a better angle for pitches, particularly the breaking ball, and makes the batter's eyes work harder to track the ball.

On the short rocker step back, the pitcher pivots and locks his foot in front of the rubber before moving forward (figure 11.3). Why the step back? The step back helps to take weight off so that the foot can turn.

To control his leg swing, the pitcher should learn to scrape or rub his pickup leg against his anchor leg when he pivots (figure 11.4). He should use the thigh muscles to pick up the front leg to help control the leg swing and achieve proper balance.

Primary Balance Point

The balance point is actually a collection phase in which the pitcher achieves balance (figure 11.5). His head and eyes are in line. His shoulders are parallel to the ground. His lower body is loaded, and he is not overrotated. The lower half of his leg is relaxed, and he has body control.

Break Phase

In the break phase (figure 11.6), the pitcher begins his movement toward the plate. We like the pitcher to soft focus on, or gaze at, the catcher's mitt while in balance. As the pitcher starts moving forward, he takes his head

a   b   c   d

Figure 11.3 The pitcher takes a short step back *(a)*, pivots *(b)*, begins to balance *(c)*, and balances *(d)*.

Figure 11.4 The pitcher scrapes the knee of his pick-up leg against his anchor leg.

Figure 11.5 The balance point.

Figure 11.6 The break phase.

and eyes to the target and achieves fine focus on the web of the catcher's mitt. He envisions handing the ball with proper hand speed to the catcher's mitt. A consistent and proper hand break helps eliminate the rush or drift problem that all pitchers face. The lead arm, throwing arm, and stride all move in sync.

The pitcher's head plays a critical role during this phase. Teach the pitcher to keep his head over his pivot foot when he moves. This head position is crucial in helping the pitcher maintain proper balance and enables him to locate his pitches. The pitcher's eyes should be relaxed as he gazes at the catcher's mitt.

The lead arm plays a major role in the direction of the front side. Proper use of the lead arm helps the shoulders move properly and aids the pitcher in throwing on a downhill plane. He reaches, cups his glove hand, and rakes hard against his glove arm so that the glove-arm elbow helps pull the throwing-arm shoulder through.

For the throwing-arm swing, the pitcher breaks with his fingers on top of the baseball throughout the arc of the swing (figure 11.7). He directs the ball toward the offside of the second-base bag. Usually, we ask the pitcher to take the ball to second base. When the arm reaches the highest point, the pitcher cocks his wrist so that the ball faces second. He should achieve upward extension on the back side.

For the stride (figure 11.8), the pitcher steps in line toward the target with his forward (glove-side) foot. He lands with his knee inside the ball of his foot with his foot slightly closed so that the front hip does not fly out prematurely. The pitcher should stay back on the pitching rubber as long as possible to achieve the maximum downward angle.

Figure 11.7 The pitcher keeps his fingers on top of the ball.

Figure 11.8 The pitcher lands on his glove-side foot.

Secondary Power Position

The minute the pitcher's front foot hits the ground, his throwing arm stops and turns over, ready to throw the ball to the catcher (figure 11.9). It is amazing how quickly the arm stroke moves. The pitcher must have upward extension on the back side. If the elbow or throwing arm is down because the pitcher broke his hands late or prematurely drifted forward, he will push the baseball through the release phase, decreasing velocity and producing sloppy, loosely spinning breaking balls.

A proper landing enables the pitcher's front shoulder to start downward and then move toward the base. His hips will start to open at the landing. He should keep his shoulders closed so that the lower half can fire with torque. His head is still. He envisions moving his chin to the plate.

A stable landing enables the pitcher to achieve a consistent release point for all pitches in his arsenal. He is able to achieve maximum hand speed through the release phase with maximum arm arc. The pitcher can throw the ball on a downward plane, using the slope of the mound to his mechanical advantage.

Follow-Through

The follow-through, the culmination of the delivery, is crucial. A good follow-through tells the pitcher that he is in control of his delivery, with all body parts flowing in sequence (figure 11.10). The lower body has eased the tremendous torque action of the release. Because many arm injuries occur in the deceleration phases, a good follow-through is essential to keeping the pitcher's arm healthy. Finally, a good follow-through puts the pitcher in the best possible position to field balls hit back through the middle.

Pitchers should learn to analyze their pitches in a positive way. Whether his last pitch completely baffled the batter or landed 400 feet from home plate, a pitcher should be able to put it behind him and accept the next pitch as a new challenge. Good competitors have a knack for moving on to the next pitch time after time.

PITCHER DELIVERY DRILLS

We use delivery drills to help our pitchers obtain a kinesthetic feel for the mechanical movements in a proper delivery. The receiver must make his partner locate each pitch so that the pitcher can teach himself how to make release-point adjustments.

Figure 11.9 The secondary power position.

Figure 11.10 The follow-through.

Pitchers can use these delivery drills every day. They should use the drills in the outfield as part of their warm-up routine. One of the benefits is that pitchers can use these drills for all pitches. Typically, our pitchers throw to each other while warming up. The pitcher receiving the ball puts his glove up to emphasize a target and location for the throwing pitcher to hit. He can move the glove to different spots so that the throwing pitcher can work on release-point adjustments and control. In this way the throwing pitcher can learn location patterns.

These drills also teach the feel of the delivery through a sequence flowing from knee to power to glide to stride to balance. The pitcher gains a feel of the flow, rhythm, and tempo, helping to ensure proper mechanics and soundness of delivery.

Knee Drill

Purpose: To emphasize upper-body technique.

Procedure:

1. Pitchers break into pairs and move to the outfield. The pitchers kneel on the pivot-leg knee with the stride foot pointed toward the target.
2. The pitcher runs through his delivery for each pitch from the kneeling position, concentrating on upper-body mechanics.

Coaching Points: Check the motion of the lead arm and the throwing-arm stroke.

Figure 11.11 Knee drill.

a

b

Power

Purpose: To emphasize lower-body technique.

Procedure:

1. The pitcher stands with the stride leg knee inside the ball of his foot, as though he has completed his stride.
2. The pitcher completes the pitch; letting his lead arm work properly, he feels upward extension of his throwing arm and the push from the back side.

Coaching Points: Check to make sure that the pitcher shifts his weight from back to front. Check his stride leg and make sure that his back hip comes over his front hip. Finish with proper shoulder rotation, chest over lead leg, and back heel to the sky.

Figure 11.12 Power drill.

a   b

Glide-to-Stride Drill

Purpose: To help the pitcher feel the transferring process and to control his delivery when movement from back to front starts to occur.

Procedure:

1. The pitcher prepares a glide to stride step with a proper stance.
2. As he completes the pitch, the pitcher focuses on the transition from the glide to the stride, controlling his follow-through.

a   b

Figure 11.13 Glide-to-Stride drill.

Figure 11.14 Balance drill.

Coaching Points: The pitcher should feel the weight transfer from back to front, which helps the lead arm, the throwing-arm stroke, and the stride landing to work properly. This drill can also help pitchers work on quickness to the plate from the stretch position.

Balance Drill

Purpose: To emphasize the collection phases of the delivery.

Procedure:
1. The pitcher moves through his delivery cycle, then collects when he reaches the balance phase.
2. After holding his balance for a few seconds, he completes his delivery.

Coaching Points: This drill shows the importance of a consistent hand break. The pitcher should break the hand in the middle of the body. The chin and head are in line. The front knee is over the back knee, which is over the ball of the back foot. This foot is positioned in front of and against the pitching rubber. The pitcher should load but not over rotate.

Full Delivery

Purpose: To have the pitcher flow through his full delivery.

Procedure:
1. The pitcher moves through each phase of the delivery.
2. Critique each pitch and watch for form breaks.
3. Have the pitcher work through every pitch in his arsenal.

Dry Drill

Purpose: To fix a specific delivery flaw. In this drill, the pitcher does not use a baseball.

Procedure:
1. The pitcher moves through each phase of his delivery, only without a baseball.
2. Critique each pitch and watch for form breaks.

Coaching Points: Work on only one flaw at a time.

Clap Drill

Purpose: To develop rhythm and control during the full delivery.

Procedure:
1. This drill can be done with or without a baseball, and can be done from the mound or in the outfield.
2. The pitcher runs through his full delivery, moving smoothly through each phase.

Coaching Points: The Clap drill helps the pitcher learn to control his delivery and develop rhythm. Use the drill with or without the baseball.

12

Changing Speeds

Courtesy of Mississippi State University

Becoming a good hitter requires a lot of work, and much of it is devoted to timing and rhythm. When a pitcher changes speeds, he disrupts the batter's timing. Changing speeds simply means varying the velocity of the pitches. A pitcher changes velocity in two ways:

1. by varying the speed of his fastball or
2. by using different pitches.

The most common way to change speeds is to vary the velocity of the fastball. We use a fastball, a batting-practice fastball, and a true straight change, all of which use backspin. We have our pitchers play catch using the different grips so that they feel comfortable with each. We also have them throw long-distance change-ups to maintain arm speed.

The second way to change speeds is to use different pitches. The breaking ball is a change-of-speed pitch because it is slower than the fastball. With the breaking ball, the axis of rotation changes from backspin to topspin. The topspin causes the ball to change planes.

Pitchers who have above-average change-ups increase their chances of being successful. Changing speeds disrupts the hitter's timing of the pitch and is a critical component to getting good hitters out.

LEARNING TO CHANGE SPEEDS

Changing speeds does not necessarily mean throwing a true straight change. Simply backing off the fastball produces a sufficient change in speed. We often refer to this pitch as a batting-practice (BP) fastball. When a pitcher throws BP, have the shagger count the number of outs batters make. You will be amazed at the large number of outs that are recorded. The BP fastball can be a simple, effective way for a pitcher, especially a younger pitcher, to change speeds.

A true straight change is a tough pitch to master. Young pitchers find it difficult to maintain arm speed and locate the pitch. When a pitcher is first learning to throw a straight change, most of his change-ups will miss high to the arm side or be horsed in the dirt. Pitchers must practice the different grips (see figure 12.1).

We have our pitchers play catch with change-up grips so that they feel comfortable with the grip and throwing action. We also play long toss with change-up grips to help ensure arm speed.

THROWING THE QUICK BREAKING BALL

We define the breaking ball as a change-of-planes pitch. A pitcher throws a breaking ball by imparting a topspin, which he can accomplish with a change in grip. Our plan includes five types of breaking balls—curve, slider, cut fastball, slurve, and split.

Curve

The curveball spins opposite to the rotation of the fastball. The ball breaks sharply in a down or drop movement pattern. The grip is important (figure 12.2). We teach a finger-down, thumb-up release point.

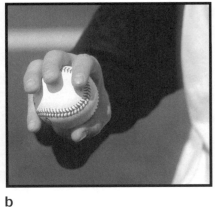

a   b   c

Figure 12.1 The change-up: *(a)* three-finger grip; *(b)* palm grip; *(c)* O.K. grip.

Figure 12.2 The curveball.

a   b

Slider

The slider breaks away from the arm side with a break that is quicker and later than the break of a curveball. The slider, also known as a 6 × 6 breaking ball, is thrown much harder than a curveball and is usually easier to control. We use an off-center grip and try to C-cut the baseball with a finger-down, thumb-up action to create the tight slider spin (figure 12.3).

The pitcher must be careful when throwing this pitch with the fingers down and the thumb up. A late, quick break is most effective. Most young pitchers want to see the pitch break, so they let the fingers get too far outside the ball, which can create elbow problems. The pitcher should stop if he feels soreness in his elbow.

Cut Fastball

The cut fastball is similar to a slider but usually stays on the same plane. The ball can be held slightly off center (figure 12.4). To achieve the off-center grip, many pitchers place the thumb under the first finger in a four-seam fastball grip. The finger action at the release point creates a movement pattern away from the arm

Figure 12.3 The slider.

Figure 12.4 The cut fastball.

side with a late break similar to that of a fastball. The pitcher releases the ball at the outer back side of the baseball.

Figure 12.5 The slurve.

Slurve

The slurve (figure 12.5) is a cross between a true curveball and a slider. Most young pitchers throw this type of breaking ball. It has curveball rotation but breaks at an angle away from the arm side. The pitch can be very effective, particularly when thrown hard. The slurve does not break laterally as much as the curveball does, so the hitter has less time to check his swing. Again, we teach a fingers-down, thumb-up release point to create topspin.

Split

We also categorize the split (figure 12.6) as a breaking ball because true splits have downward action. In essence, the split becomes a breaking ball, and the pitcher may not need another type of breaking ball. Although I have seen no surefire documentation that the split creates elbow problems, pitchers should stop throwing it if they experience elbow tenderness.

The split can be an outstanding addition to a pitcher's arsenal, and most find it simple to grip. The pitcher spreads the first and second fingers outside the two seams. He should start with the thumb in the middle and then experiment with an off-center grip. The pitch usually moves opposite the thumb. If the size of the pitcher's fingers allows it, he can spread the fingers around the U seams.

A pitcher should generally arm himself with only one type of breaking ball and perfect it. The length of the fingers usually dictates the most comfortable and efficient breaking-ball grip.

LOCATING THE BREAKING BALL

Most young pitchers need to learn to tighten or shorten the break of the pitch so that they can locate the ball in the strike zone and throw the curveball in the dirt. A breaking ball is much more efficient when located down.

Figure 12.6 The split.

We all know that hanging breaking balls get hit a long way. Normally, the tighter, quicker breaking ball is more effective. When a young pitcher moves to the next level (for example, from high school to college), one of the major adjustments he must make is to tighten up his breaking ball. Most good hitters learn to take the pitch if a pitcher shows that he cannot throw it for a strike.

In our pitch sequences, we describe the breaking balls as extra, control, or dirt. The extra breaking ball is the pitcher's best breaking ball. It moves away from the arm side, and the pitcher generally uses it as his strikeout pitch.

The control breaking ball is a pitch that will be called a strike if the batter takes it. Generally, the pitcher throws this pitch when he is behind in the count. The hitter usually takes this pitch because he is looking for a fastball to hit a long way. Some refer to this pitch as a "hit me" breaking ball.

The dirt breaking ball is a pitch that must bounce. Ideally, it bounces right behind the plate. The pitcher throws it as a strikeout pitch or as a pitch to expand the upper half of the strike zone. When the catcher signals this pitch, he knows he must block it.

In our pitch-calling sequence, the catcher signals what type of breaking ball the pitcher should throw. We feel this eliminates any doubt in the pitcher's mind of the purpose of that particular breaking ball.

Locating Pitches

When pitchers start to struggle in a game, many try to throw harder pitches. Throwing harder usually causes the ball to straighten out, and the batter hits it harder. Good pitchers learn to back down and locate. The pitches move more, usually resulting in more ground balls and giving the defense a chance to make plays. Once a pitcher understands that balls hit in fair territory become outs most of the time, he becomes much more successful.

Locating the pitch simply means throwing the ball to a specific target. Many pitchers assume that location pertains only to the fastball, but we feel that all pitches (sliders, curveballs, splits, and changes) must be located. The specific target is the catcher's mitt. Our pitchers use a two-stage focusing process—a soft focus and then a fine focus—to zero in on the catcher's mitt.

The position of the pitcher's head can be a major factor in the location of the pitch. We prefer a still, quiet head. The head position also affects balance.

In his initial stance and setup, the pitcher should relax his eyes. When he leaves the balance position, his head and eyes pick up the specific target—the catcher's mitt. We refer to this as soft focus.

We teach our pitchers to think that the eyes can route the pitch. We often describe this as fine focus, a concentration on the web of the catcher's mitt.

LOCATING THE FASTBALL

We believe in pitching with a located fastball. Our pitchers use the two-seam grip and the four-seam grip. We generally locate the two-seam fastball down in the strike zone and the four-seam fastball up in the strike zone. This concept takes advantage of the natural movement created by a two-seam fastball (sink or lateral run; figure 13.1) and the four-seam fastball (lift or longer path on the same plane; figure 13.2).

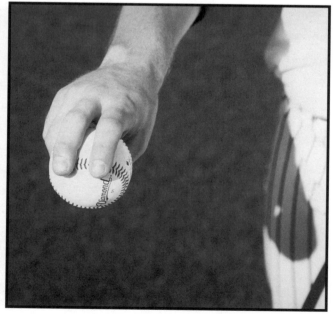

Figure 13.1 The two-seam fastball.

Figure 13.2 The four-seam fastball.

Each of our pitchers must understand what it means to read his run, to follow the natural movement patterns of the fastball in flight. The fastball will generally move in one of three ways—sink, lateral run, or lift.

The pitcher must also understand that location is where the catcher receives the pitch at the end of the run. The pitch will move from the release point through its flight to the location at the plate.

Second, we use the terms *arm side* and *away from the arm side* (see figures 13.3 and 13.4). Our pitcher must be able to locate his fastball away from the arm side. Typically, a fastball located arm side will move more than one located away from the arm side. Our pitcher must first master location away from the arm side for two major reasons:

1. Pitching away from the arm side is more difficult to master because the pitcher must hold the ball longer. Doing this ensures that he has a solid delivery.

2. The fastball located away from the arm side typically does not move as much, so location is more of a factor.

We start left-handed pitchers in the same mind-set; however, left-handed pitchers win with a greater degree of arm-side location patterns.

Figure 13.3 Away from the arm side: RHP to RH batter, location down and away.

Figure 13.4 Arm side: RHP to RH batter, location in.

TEACHING PITCHERS TO LOCATE THE PITCH

When instructing your pitchers in a mechanical phase, do not emphasize location. Teach one point at a time. More often than not, improving one area will straighten out two or three other areas in the delivery.

When instructing in location patterns, demand location. Do not bombard the pitcher's mind by asking him to make adjustments in his delivery. Granted, the flaw in his delivery is probably the reason he is not precise with location. Ask him to make release-point adjustments to locate the pitch.

During practice, pitchers do not always throw to the catcher but instead play catch and do delivery drills with other pitchers. Thus the receiver (the person catching the ball) during the drill has as much responsibility as the thrower. He puts up his glove to give the pitcher a specific target. This forces the pitcher to learn and understand release-point adjustments. Release-point adjustments become the way that the pitcher achieves control. Second, the receiver moves the target to force the thrower to make release-point adjustments. The pitcher must understand that he needs to make only minor adjustments to control his pitches. A common fault is to make a major adjustment. I often use the following example:

A pitcher is throwing in a game. He throws the first pitch letter high to the batter. The second pitch is in the same location—ball 2. The pitcher has a 2-0 count working against him. He tells himself to make an adjustment. The next pitch bounces at home plate. Did he make an adjustment? Yes, but the release-point adjustment was excessive. A pitcher must remember to make minor adjustments to help his control because the ball is traveling to a specific target (catcher's mitt) over a long distance (60 feet, 6 inches).

PRACTICING LOCATING THE PITCH

Pitchers work on location and adjustments during their warm-up delivery drills (see chapter 11). During delivery drills, the receiving pitcher moves his glove, forcing the throwing pitcher to make release-point adjustments to locate the pitch. During bullpen workouts and batting practice, the catcher moves his glove around, forcing the pitcher to locate pitches. The coach can help the pitcher improve his pitch location by correcting delivery flaws and teaching him to make adjustments and corrections.

Holding Runners

Keeping runners close to the bases is an area of the game I become excited about. Keeping runners close requires hard work and a commitment to practice daily. Pitchers must understand and mentally process running counts and situations. Obviously, some pitchers will be more adept at controlling runners, but every pitcher can improve on his stretch mechanics and various moves.

In his book *Pitching* (1972, Contemporary Books, Chicago), Bob Shaw, an outstanding major-league pitcher and coach, and in my mind a brilliant teacher, teaches pitchers to remember the 1, 2, 3s:

1. As the catcher returns the ball, the pitcher should check each base runner.
2. Stand on the pitching rubber to get the signal.
3. Pitch or pick.

Following these simple steps will reduce the runner's lead by six inches at the start of every play because the runner and the opposing coach know that you will pick. How many safe or out calls are decided by half a foot?

Emphasize and work on stretch delivery mechanics so that the pitcher feels comfortable throwing all his pitches from the stretch. In his prepitch plan, the pitcher must consider his defensive role in pickoff attempts, in covering bunts, in the first-and-third defense, or in backing up bases. After mentally processing his defensive role, he must process the specific pitch and location.

We predetermine all our pickoff attempts. We do not want our pitchers to focus in two areas at once. I feel strongly that this simple plan has helped our pitching staff in both pickoff attempt location and quality of pitch and location to home plate. We ask left-handed pitchers to read the runner at first base for one-way steal body language. If the pitcher cannot refocus his mind to the pitch plan, he simply steps off.

CLASSIFYING RUNNERS

The next part of our plan is to classify the runners at first base and second base. The outcome of a steal attempt depends on three numbers—pitcher time sets, catcher throwing time, and base-runner running time. We classify runners into three types—the runner, the count runner, and no runner—based on the scouting report, the runner's stats and position, the batting order, and simply by observation and timing.

The runner is a base stealer. He is successful most of the time. Our goal is to make the steal as tough as possible, but we understand that he will be successful in some steal attempts. This is not a defeatist attitude but a realistic one. Our goal is to have strike one at the completion of the play. More often than not, the batter will take the pitch. The pitcher should not let the runner start a big inning by getting behind the batter in the count.

The count runner is the base stealer who tries to pick a breaking ball or change to make his steal attempt. Scout the third-base coach and read his signal system. Read the runner's body language. Use the pick when the count dictates a breaking ball or off-speed pitch. We must throw out this runner to be successful in close games or against teams who force the running game. Locate the picks!

For a no runner, simply force the runner to stop and not get a walking lead. Caution the middle infielders and catcher to be aware of the delayed steal.

UNDERSTANDING THE PICKOFF

Our pitchers must understand the mental concepts and physically work the pickoff. When an opposing runner reaches first, we are going to pick, and the opposition soon knows it.

The pitcher must be able to hold the ball to a three-second count when his hand bottoms out in the stretch position. The best base stealers tell us that the pitcher who can hold the ball and pick or pitch is the toughest to steal against.

We define pickoff attempts as follows: a pickoff is a located pitch with short arm action located 24 inches over the inside corner of the bag. We believe this precision is necessary for success. Thus, both right-handed and left-handed pitchers must be able to do the following:

- Throw the comfort pick, the standard reliable pick.
- Hold the ball and pitch. *Hold* means a three-second-plus count. Our pitchers practice this by counting when the hands set or bottom out (for example, they count one thousand one, one thousand two, one thousand three, then pick or pitch).
- Hold the ball and pick. The pitcher holds the ball for three seconds or longer and locates a pick to the base.
- Throw the quick pitch. When the hand bottoms out, the pitcher moves quickly to throw the called pitch.
- Hold, hold, step off. The pitcher checks the runner's body language. A flinch will indicate what to do on the next pitch.
- Hold, hold, hold until the batter steps out of the box.
- Pitch out. Pitchers work with the catcher in the bullpen at least three times a week. With some pitchers, we incorporate the pitchout into the pregame ritual.
- Pitch around. The pitcher works on this skill in bullpen sessions. He does not simply throw breaking balls. Most pitchers can locate the fastball more accurately.
- Use the intentional walk, not only when rules dictate a free base. Pitchers work on the technique and team defense in practice. Pitchers must incorporate this into bullpen sessions two times per week using a four-seam fastball grip.

We work hard with our pitchers to improve their time sets to the plate. I believe a pitcher can improve his time set without losing velocity, spin, or rotation on his breaking ball. Some pitchers can be quicker than others. The body physique of the individuals play a role. But with work, each pitcher can improve. We use the stopwatch and radar gun to monitor work. We incorporate a signal system with our catcher that lets the pitcher know to be quicker. If you are opposed to the idea of glide to stride, simply do not require it from your pitchers.

In the glide to stride, many pitchers pick up only their front knees on the slide step. The problem with doing this is that the throwing arm doesn't have time to go down, back, and up. The coaching point that we teach is that the pitcher must take his front knee to his back knee and abbreviate the height of the lift. This simple action lets the arm stroke work properly to maintain velocity and enables the pitcher to spin the breaking ball correctly.

We ask pitchers to deliver the ball to home plate within 1.3 to 1.5 seconds. Many are much quicker. The timing starts with the pitcher's first move and stops when the catcher receives the pitch.

Some of our left-handed pitchers also work on a slide step and a slide-step pick. For the slide step the pitcher abbreviates his front-leg lift by keeping his leg closer to the ground. He directs his front knee toward his back knee at an angle. He shifts his weight to the back side and quickens his arm action. The key for the pitcher is to be quick without losing velocity, accuracy, or spin rotation for breaking pitches.

PICKOFF MOVES

Pickoffs are important in helping a team control the running game. Picks are also effective in testing the offense in bunt situations. Pitchers must work daily on their pickoff moves.

Emphasize three major points when teaching the pickoff:

1. Quick feet and quick upper body
2. Short arm action
3. Accurate location

All three points are vital for both left-handed and right-handed pitchers.

Right-Handed Pitchers

The pitcher's feet are about shoulder-width apart. His knees are slightly flexed. The pitcher's shoulders and hips are level, and his weight is equally distributed. We refer to this as good athletic position, a position from which the pitcher can move quickly. We like our pitchers to set their hands as quickly as possible to eliminate wasted movement.

Many coaches teach the pitcher to set initially with hands high. If you teach your pitcher to do this, I think it is important for the pitcher to develop moves (a) from the top, (b) on the way up or down, and (c) at the bottom.

We like our pitchers to set quickly and pick from the set position (figure 14.1). They must work on this continually. When the pitcher's hands come set, he wants to keep in motion with a hand bounce and then pick or pitch. Holding completely still is difficult. The internal body system wants to continue the movement with rhythm. As his hands set, the pitcher tucks his chin to his shoulder, varies the time set, and picks or pitches.

I like our pitcher to predetermine whether he is pitching or picking. This thought processing enables a pitcher to commit mentally and then physically to the motor movement of the skill. He can clearly visualize the located pickoff or the fastball down and away.

The actual move is a jump, pivot, and step. We stress upper-body quickness first because the knees are flexed. We want the glove arm to go up and take the throwing arm to the ear with the palm facing down. This will shorten the arm stroke so that the pitcher can get the ball in the air more quickly. The pitcher jumps, keeping his feet close to the ground, steps to first, and delivers the pick with a short, crisp, accurate throw (figure 14.2).

a   b   c

Figure 14.1   A right-handed pitcher setting from the stretch.

A common mistake pitchers make is dropping the throwing arm below the belt buckle. This movement elongates the path of the throwing arm. He can push the arm back on purpose, however, to set up the quick move. We refer to this as a change-up pick. Another common mistake pitchers make is jumping too high.

Left-Handed Pitchers

Our left-handers think more about deception. Time and hard work are required to develop a good move.

Left-handers use an initial set similar to that used by right-handers. The advantage that the left-hander has is that he can look directly at the base runner on first. As his hand comes set, we want him to read the body language of the runner. As he picks up his leg, the pitcher can see easily if the runner breaks on his first movement.

The pitcher must control his leg swing by balancing his knee over the ball of his foot. His knee and foot should be as close to vertical as possible and always on the same plane. Once he has achieved the primary balance position, he can pitch or pick (figure 14.3).

Many left-handed pitchers give away the pick by their head action. If the pitcher's head goes home, he will pick; when he continues to watch the runner, he will pitch.

Figure 14.2 The pickoff move to first (right-handed pitcher).

a

b

c

d

e

f

a

b

c

Figure 14.3 The pickoff move to first (left-handed pitcher).

The pitcher needs to control his head action. When the knee reaches the highest point, the pitcher tucks his chin to his front shoulder.

The next phase is a homeward drift with the break phase occurring exactly as if the pitcher is delivering the ball to home. The shoulder turn or arm stroke often point directly toward third base, giving away the pickoff attempt.

We tell pitchers to think and act homeward and use the same homeward lead arm action. They start the leg swing homeward, then step toward first base in what most people call the 45-degree angle.

Consistency and hard work will enable a left-handed pitcher to pick off his share of base runners. In addition, a left-hander with good technique will force many opposing coaches to abandon the running game.

Another move for the left-handed pitcher is the quick step move. As his hand starts to come set, he picks up his left foot and puts it behind the pitching rubber as the base runner extends his lead. This move can be effective against runners who take big leads or who like to jump back and forth.

PICKOFF MOVES TO SECOND

Pickoff plays to second base are important in a defensive scheme because many base runners will attempt to steal third.

The first aspect is to determine and recognize whether the shortstop or second baseman has bag coverage.

We like to give a signal on each pitch so that everyone in the infield tunes in as the catcher returns the ball to the pitcher. The pitcher turns and looks at the middle infielder, who relays a quick series of signals. Doing this takes only a few seconds and lets everyone know when the pitcher will pitch and whether a predetermined play is on. Our defense can thus be set before the pitcher delivers the ball to the plate.

The mechanics of the pick are similar to those of the jump pickoff to first base by a right-handed pitcher. The difference is that the pitcher's feet replace each other to complete the jump turn (figure 14.4).

Figure 14.4   Pickoff move to second base (right-handed pitcher).

Most of our pitchers jump turn to the glove side. We have a few who jump turn inside or to the arm side. Simply time each pitcher and check for accuracy to determine what is best for him.

The three most common types of moves are daylight, the timing pick, and the inside pick.

Daylight

The daylight move is usually not predetermined. The middle infielder who has bag coverage sees the base runner moving aggressively into a secondary lead. The infielder sprints to the bag and shows his glove (shortstop) or bare hand (second baseman) to the pitcher. The pitcher sees this, automatically jump turns, and delivers the ball belt high to the second baseman over the inside corner of the bag. In my opinion, the infielder should predetermine as many steal attempts as possible and use a predetermined step to help the pitcher know a move is coming. We do not want to pitch with the middle infielders out of position.

Timing Pick

With the timing pick, the middle infielder signals the pitcher. Pitchers use either a count system (one thousand one, one thousand two, one thousand three, pick) or a specific number of head looks. The middle infielder breaks on a predetermined number. The pitcher delivers the ball. Some teams will break the shortstop first when the runner takes off. The second baseman breaks, and the pitcher throws the ball at that point.

Many teams will let the middle infielder who backs up the throw from the catcher catch the pickoff attempt from the pitcher. Typically, the second baseman will have bag control when a right-handed batter is at the plate. The shortstop has bag control for a left-handed batter.

Some teams will attempt a pickoff with movement by both middle infielders. The shortstop and second baseman alternate moving in and then backing out. Many runners at second base will expand their leads when one infielder moves away. When the runner takes a longer lead, the other middle infielder breaks back to the bag and receives the pickoff attempt from the pitcher.

Inside Pick

The inside pick (figure 14.5) can be effective against a runner who takes a short primary lead but extends it when the pitcher picks up his leg. The move is somewhat difficult. The pitcher picks up his front leg, pivots on his back leg, and then spins inside and picks to the middle infielder who has bag coverage.

PICKOFF MOVES TO THIRD

The leg-lift pick to third base can be effective for a right-handed pitcher to deter false breaks, a steal of home plate, or the suicide squeeze. For a left-handed pitcher, the step-off is also effective. The left-handed pitcher in his windup position simply steps back off the pitching rubber with his pivot foot and then stops and completes the throw to the third baseman.

a

b

c

d

Figure 14.5 The inside pick to second base.

The fake to third and pick at first can be effective in a third-and-one defense or against teams who like to fake steal or hit and run in these situations. The right-handed pitcher lifts his leg as if he is delivering a pitch to home plate. He steps to third base when his front foot hits the ground, then jump pivots to first base and throws to the first baseman.

PICKOFF DRILLS

We incorporate our pickoff moves into our drills daily. We practice during the warm-up period.

Two-Line Pickoff Drill

Purpose: To reinforce the techniques used in all pickoff moves.

Procedure:
1. Pitchers partner up and stand 30 feet apart in two lines in the outfield, facing each other.
2. Pitchers use all pickoff moves with their partners (figure 14.6). Either the coach or the pitcher can call which pickoff move will be used (predetermine picks).

Coaching Points: Watch for mechanical flaws and correct any errors.

Figure 14.6   The Two-Line Pickoff drill.

Triangle Picks

Purpose: To reinforce the techniques used for pickoff plays at first base, second base, and third base.

Procedure:
1. The pitchers form three groups. You need three pitchers to drill the picks at first and third base and four pitchers to drill the picks at second base. (You can use three pitchers to drill the picks at second base by predetermining

the pick and using either the short-stop or second baseman as the covering infielder.)

2. For the picks at first base, one pitcher acts as the catcher, one acts as the first baseman, and one is the pitcher. The pitcher works through his pickoff sequence, throwing both to the first baseman (figure 14.8a) and to the catcher (figure 14.8b). Simulate game conditions; pitchers should predetermine picks.

3. For the picks at second base, one pitcher acts as the shortstop, one acts as the second baseman, one acts as the catcher, and one is the pitcher. The pitcher works through his pick-off sequence, throwing to the short-stop or second baseman or to the catcher.

4. For the picks at third base, one pitcher acts as the third baseman, one acts as the catcher, and one is the pitcher. The pitcher works through his pickoff sequence, throwing both to the third baseman and to the catcher.

5. Players rotate to the different positions in their groups and then rotate groups.

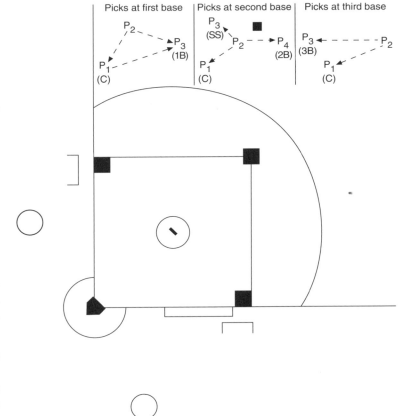

Figure 14.7 Setup for Triangle Picks.

a

b

Figure 14.8 The Triangle Picks drill.

Pitcher Fielding Plays

We think of pitcher fielding plays as momentum shifters. Pitchers must take pride in fielding their position and playing their part in team defense. Obviously, the first responsibility of a pitcher is to throw strikes. But once he delivers the ball to the plate, he can play a major role in securing an out. Like the position players on defense, the pitcher should include in his prepitch ritual an answer to the question, "If the ball is hit to me, what is my responsibility?" The pitcher's job is then to focus on the pitch and location before he toes the pitching rubber to deliver the ball to the catcher's mitt. To help the pitcher field the ball, we also work hard on infield arm action in our throwing drills. We like our pitcher to call for the ball, particularly when he is moving to first base.

Pitchers have many opportunities to field the ball, but these six are the most common pitcher fielding plays:

1. Fielding the ball hit back to the pitcher (tapped or bunted)
2. Participating in a double play
3. Participating in pop-ups
4. Covering first base
5. Backing up bases
6. Covering home plate

FIELDING THE BALL HIT BACK TO THE PITCHER

We divide the field into four fielding zones (figure 15.1)—the hop zone, the hurry zone, the flip zone, and the full-arm fake zone. Each zone relates to a specific way to field the ball. The zones can shift based on the speed of the runner, how hard or how soft the ball is batted or bunted, or the game situation—score, outs, and inning. Pitchers recognize these fielding zones and work on technique in practices and repetitions. Players must practice fielding skills, as they must most things, to develop good habits.

Hop Zone

When the ball is hit directly at the pitcher, he catches it as an infielder does on his glove side (figure 15.2). The pitcher shuffles his feet in the direction of the bag to which he is throwing (usually first base). He does not break his hands until he is prepared to throw. He just shuffles repeatedly and throws! The left-handed pitcher turns with his glove and then shuffles.

Hurry Zone

When the ball is hit away from first base or tapped with airtime, the pitcher must get the ball in the air quickly. The right-handed pitcher catches the ball in his glove on his throwing-arm side (figure 15.3). His right leg is flexed, and he does not need to step. He just flexes and throws. The left-handed pitcher steps over the ball, fields it, and then throws to first base.

For bouncing balls or balls rolling hard, we teach our pitchers to use the glove to field the ball. On balls rolling slowly, pitchers should use a barehanded, full-hand grab underneath the ball and a fine-tune grip to throw it. If the ball is not rolling, pitchers should use a barehanded, full-hand grab on top of the ball.

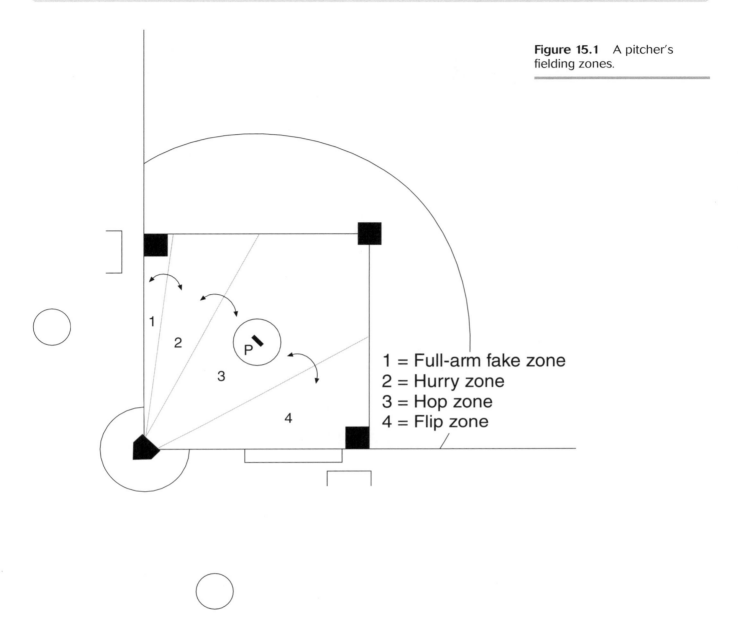

Figure 15.1 A pitcher's fielding zones.

1 = Full-arm fake zone
2 = Hurry zone
3 = Hop zone
4 = Flip zone

If the pitcher is not sure whether the ball is in the hurry zone or the hop zone, he should approach the play as if he is in the hurry zone then adjust to the hop zone if necessary. For example, a fast runner bunts the ball to the third-base side. The pitcher approaches the ball in hurry fashion and secures it. As he starts to throw, he sees the runner fall. He simply shuffles twice and then throws. This is how a hurry play becomes a hop play.

Flip Zone

The flip zone covers balls hit to the first-base side of the mound (figure 15.4). When a pitcher catches the ball moving toward first base, we want him to sprint toward the inside corner of the bag. He must always call for the ball when he is sure he can glove it. When he recognizes that the first baseman has bag control, he shuffles and flips the ball to him. The flip is just like the flip that the shortstop or second baseman

a

b

c

Figure 15.2 Fielding the ball in the hop zone.

a   b   c

d   e

Figure 15.3 Fielding the ball in the hurry zone.

a

b

c

d

e

Figure 15.4 Fielding the ball in the flip zone.

uses. If the first baseman false breaks and cannot get back to the base, the pitcher should beat the runner to the bag.

Full-Arm Fake Zone

The pitcher, corner infielders, and catcher must know how balls will roll down the foul lines. When in doubt, they should always let it roll. At times, however, the ball stays fair and the pitcher has no chance to throw out the runner. We practice the full-arm fake and look to another base (figure 15.5). If the back base runner makes

a

b

c

d

Figure 15.5 Fielding the ball in the full-arm fake zone.

a big turn, the fielder may be able to turn a negative into a positive. A fielder might also use the full-arm fake if he bobbles the ball and cannot throw out the runner. He should not give up but use the full-arm fake to make something happen!

PARTICIPATING IN A DOUBLE PLAY

The pitcher starts to turn the double play. On a ball hit back to him, the pitcher starts the play by fielding the ball and throwing it chest high to the middle infielder over the inside corner of the bag. The middle infielder completes the double play. The best way I have heard it explained is simply, "Get a hard out at second base." The pitcher should shuffle or crow hop. He should not break his hands until he is prepared to throw. The shuffle gives the covering middle infielder time to get to the bag. The shuffle also aligns the pitcher so that his directional side is in position to throw the ball accurately. Remember to practice home-to-first double plays (pitcher to catcher to first baseman).

PARTICIPATING IN POP-UPS

When a baseball is hit in the air and stays in the ballpark, the defense must catch it. Ideally, your best fielder should have priority. In many cases, that person may be the pitcher. The coaching point is simple: catch it!

We let our pitchers catch pop-ups. We use a priority system with all infielders and call the ball at the highest point. Even if your pitcher is low in the priority system, he should continue to practice catching pop-ups. He must catch low-trajectory pop-ups in front of the mound or in foul territory.

COVERING FIRST BASE

The pitcher must always break toward first base when a ball is hit to his left. He must make it a habit. His goal is to beat the fastest runners all the time and then adjust to the slower runners.

We draw a line from the pitching rubber to the inside corner of the first-base bag. Our pitcher should never cross that line to the second-base side. The pitcher or first baseman quickly calls, "Ball, ball!" The other player goes to the first base bag. During drill work, we make the first baseman adjust positions in depth.

The pitcher takes a direct route of five to seven feet in front of the first base bag and runs parallel to the baseline (figure 15.6). This enables the pitcher to square his shoulders to the first baseman. The pitcher shows his glove. He controls his body, anticipating a bad ball, but does not decelerate early. He catches the ball high in his glove. Looking at the base, the pitcher touches it with his right foot. He shuffles his feet and prepares to throw (i.e., to home plate on a two-out wheel play from second base).

If the pitcher has not received the ball by the time he touches the bag, he stops. If he has time, he becomes the first baseman. If he does not have time, he sees the ball and steps to it in a stretch.

We never want our pitchers to step in the middle of the base or cross the base line. That is the runner's territory. The only time we allow pitchers to cross the base line is when the ball caroms off the first baseman into foul territory. If the pitcher has time, he shuffles to the outside third of the bag and stays out of the runner's path.

On 3-6-1 double plays, the pitcher must take a direct path to the bag. He squares his shoulders to second base and stretches when he sees the ball.

BACKING UP BASES

We must always have a back line of defense. Initially, our outfielders back up bases and plays. But when the outfielders are busy in the outfield, the pitcher becomes the last line of defense. He must back up the play, always assuming that he is needed. He should position himself as deep as the playing field permits in the trajectory line of the throw and then adjust in.

Backing up bases completes the play for a pitcher. The pitcher who makes the correct backup play can change the outcome of a close game!

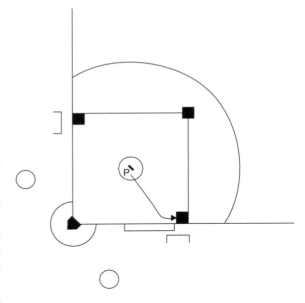

Figure 15.6 Pitcher covering first base.

COVERING HOME PLATE

On a wild pitch or passed ball, the pitcher has the responsibility to cover home. First, the pitcher points out the ball to the catcher. (He must also point out all foul balls to the catcher.) Second, he communicates where the ball is rolling:

- One—first-base side
- Three—third-base side
- Four—home plate
- Back—the ball is rolling away; it is deep
- Down—in the circle or below the catcher or umpire

The pitcher runs hard to home plate. He positions his foot in line with the third-base bag for safety. He gives the runner the back outside part of the plate on which to slide. As he nears the plate, the pitcher calls the catcher by name. He catches the ball in his glove, makes a sweeping tag, and keeps his throwing hand away from sliding cleats.

PITCHER FIELDING DRILLS

Pitcher's Pepper

Purpose: To improve pitchers' fielding ability and technique.

Procedure:
1. Pitchers gather in the outfield. Either a pitcher or the coach can act as the hitter.

2. Simulate plays that arise during a game. Practice fielding plays, backing up bases, and pickoff moves.

Coaching Points: Watch for proper fielding and throwing technique.

Cover First Base

Purpose: To improve pitchers' ability to cover first base.

Procedure:
1. Pitchers line up behind the pitching mound. First basemen line up near first base.
2. Using a fungo bat, the coach hits the ball to the first-base side of the mound.
3. The first baseman fields the ball and flips it to the pitcher covering first base.
4. After completing the play, the pitcher and first baseman move to the back of their lines.

Coaching Points: Use this drill to teach proper mechanics in covering first base to establish teamwork and communication between the pitchers and first basemen.

Double Play

Purpose: To reinforce the pitcher's role in starting the double play.

Procedure:
1. The first baseman, second baseman, shortstop, and pitcher take their positions in the infield.
2. The coach or another player hits a ground ball to the pitcher.
3. The pitcher fields the ball and throws to the shortstop or second baseman to start the double play.
4. The pitcher throws chest high over the inside corner of second base.
5. Practice the pitcher to catcher to first baseman double play.

First-Base, Second-Base, Third-Base, Home-Plate Pepper

Purpose: To practice gamelike situations.

Procedure:
1. In the outfield, the pitchers split into four groups of three pitchers. Each group will need one other player or a coach to act as the batter.
2. For the first group, one pitcher acts as the first baseman. In the second group, one pitcher acts as

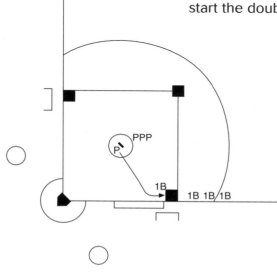

Figure 15.7 Setup for Cover First Base drill.

the shortstop. In the third group, one pitcher acts as the third baseman. For the fourth group, one pitcher acts as the catcher.

3. Simulate different game situations. Have each pitcher work through all his pitches.

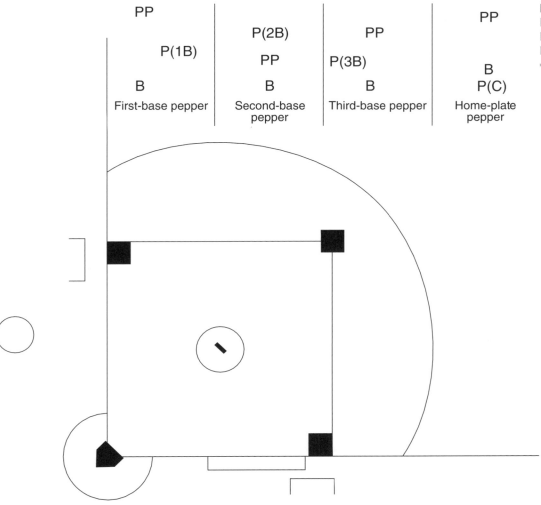

PP		P(2B)	PP		PP
P(1B)		PP	P(3B)		B
B		B	B		P(C)
First-base pepper		Second-base pepper	Third-base pepper		Home-plate pepper

Figure 15.8 Setup for First-Base, Second-Base, Third-Base, Home-Plate Pepper.

Pitcher's Fielding Plays Practice

Purpose: To practice gamelike situations.

Procedure:

1. During a scrimmage or practice game, have the pitcher practice different game situations.

2. Watch for proper execution of fielding ground balls, fielding fly balls, backing up bases, and participating in double plays.

Catching Technique

When I think about a catcher's development, the first thing that comes to mind is how he handles himself and the pitcher during bullpen workouts. The second thing that comes to mind is that a good catcher makes an average pitching staff much better. Unfortunately, the opposite is also true. When a pitcher is afraid to throw his breaking ball in the dirt with two strikes or with runners on base, particularly third base, negative things usually happen. You see a pitching staff that starts to overthrow and thus is always pitching behind in the count. You also see more walks.

Good catchers have the will and ability to keep balls from getting by them. A good catcher loves to put on his gear and wear it around. He takes great pride in letting everyone know he is the team's catcher. He works to command respect from each pitcher and must be the liaison between the pitching coach and the pitching staff.

I have been blessed to be around scores of outstanding student-athletes and baseball players. Many of the guys I have become closest to are catchers, particularly our bullpen catchers. They have special qualities and, in my mind, are the most valuable players of our pitching staff.

In this chapter, I will highlight the major areas and qualities it takes to be a catcher.

Figure 16.1 Make sure the catcher is close enough to touch the batter's back.

STANCE

We like to break the stance into three distinct areas:

1. the signal stance,
2. the shift to the receiving stance with no one on base, and
3. the shift to the receiving stance with runners on base.

I also believe the two-strike stance should be addressed. Blocking the pitch becomes an issue.

Signal Stance

A first-rate catcher gives signals with conviction. He makes the pitcher feel confident that he has called the correct pitch and location. A good catcher controls the pitcher's tempo.

Many catchers set up too far from the batter. The catcher should be able to reach up and touch the batter's back (figure 16.1). The catcher should be careful of a batter who has a big loop; the umpire could call interference if the catcher sets up too closely.

In the signal stance (figure 16.2), the catcher's heels are upright and together. The back shoulder is flat. The catcher has eye contact with the pitcher, but he watches the batter to make sure he isn't peeking, trying to steal the signal.

To send the signal, the catcher tucks his right forearm. He extends his fingers into his crotch area, being careful not to drop his fingers so far that they expose the signals (figure 16.3). The glove hides the signals from the third-base coach. The catcher should avoid letting his elbow fly, which can give away location. His knees protect the signals from the base runners.

The signal system should be clear and well defined. The pitch and specific location are important. We also signal picks when runners are on base. Having a false shake is important. You may consider a no-pitch signal if a pickoff play is on. When runners are on base, you should use some type of multiple signal system. Practice this in the bullpen and use it in practices or scrimmages when no one is on base. You may consider having a signal for a curveball that will bounce, which we refer to as a dirt breaking ball.

Shift to the Receiving Position With No One on Base

The catcher shuffles his feet to get in receiving position (figure 16.4). Many catchers give away the pitch and location by awkwardly shifting or moving forward on certain pitches. We like our catchers to be in position to handle the low, away pitches (from a right-handed pitcher).

The catcher's feet are apart. His toes can point outward, enabling his tail and body to stay low. He gives the pitcher a flat glove target with the glove elbow outside his knee and his glove fingers pointing up.

The subject of what to do with the throwing hand is always a popular discussion. Four common methods are used: keeping the hand behind the back, keeping the hand inside the thigh, wrapping the bare hand, or rolling the bare hand into a fist around the glove with the inside fingers. Figure 16.5 shows the catcher set in the receiving position with his hand behind his back.

We prefer the two-hand method with the thumb inside the wrap of the fingers. We feel it is safer because it protects the catcher's hand on a foul tip.

As the pitcher releases the ball, we like the catcher to do one of two things:

1. Relax the glove hand. The top of the mitt faces the pitcher, and the catcher is free to move to the location of the pitch.

2. Point the glove thumb to the sky upon release. Most refer to this as a half moon.

Figure 16.2 The signal stance.

Figure 16.3 The catcher sends the signals.

Figure 16.4 The catcher shuffles to the receiving position.

Figure 16.5 Catcher set with his throwing hand behind his back.

Shift to the Receiving Position With Runners on Base

The catcher must put his body in a position to receive the pitch and block or throw. The catcher elevates his tail. His back is flat. He is now in better position to drop or let his knees replace his feet to block the pitch (figure 16.6).

FRAMING THE PITCH

An outstanding receiver catches a pitched ball in a way that is more likely to produce a strike call. The catcher's relationship with the umpire is also important. The catcher should receive the pitch in the strike zone and keep it there. I like the phrase "Stick the pitch."

The catcher can funnel, or frame, a close pitch. Any part of the ball determines a strike. Good receivers have a wonderful way of receiving the close pitch so that it results in a strike call. Poor catchers take the ball out of the zone, making a close pitch look farther away. Put simply, if the ball flows

Figure 16.6 The receiving position with runners on base.

through any part of the strike zone, we want the umpire to call it a strike. Framing a pitch teaches a catcher good receiving discipline. Figure 16.7 shows four different ways to frame a pitch.

BLOCKING

The catcher must have in his mind that he will not let the ball get by him. His knees replace his feet. He does not catch the ball; he blocks it with his body (figure 16.8). He tucks his chin and rolls his shoulder. His arms and glove extend to the ground to block the hole. The chest protector helps soften the dirt ball. Ideally, the ball falls to the plate. The catcher bare hands the top of the ball and gets in position to throw.

On pitches that are outside the zone but are close and blockable, the catcher tries to force his shoulders to angle behind the plate to keep the ball in front of him (figure 16.9). The catcher understands that dirt curveballs angle back with spin. Some catchers employ a one-knee block on pitches to the glove side.

When pitches are clearly outside the block zone (three balls outside the plate), the catcher uses a block pick. Catchers sometimes have a tendency to pick pitches or glove pitches instead of blocking them.

Drills and hard work are important in learning to block successfully. We practice blocking with rag balls, tennis balls, and flexi-balls. These balls typically bounce differently, however, so we use real baseballs as well. You can use football arm pads during some drills to protect unprotected areas.

Figure 16.7 Framing the pitch: *(a)* up; *(b)* down; *(c)* away (right-handed batter and right-handed pitcher); *(d)* method #1 in, glove outside.

Figure 16.8 The catcher blocks the ball with his body.

a

b

Figure 16.9 Blocking at an angle: *(a)* to the right; *(b)* to the left.

a

THROWING

All our position players work hard on our throwing-drill program. Catchers use an abbreviated or shortened arm stroke to get the ball in the air quickly. Proper footwork helps get the body in a balanced position to throw the ball accurately and with the best time set. We time our catchers and grade them on accuracy. We time them between pitches of each inning of a game. When we are scrimmaging and we know the steal is on, we also grade and time.

Catchers must understand that most bases are stolen on the break off the pitcher. When a runner steals, the catcher's job is to throw his best time with accuracy. That means he has done all he can! Proper receiving techniques enable the catcher to rake or center the ball. He can get his lower body in position, align his front shoulder to the target, and deliver the ball to the base with accuracy. Our catchers use a four-seam grip.

The catcher's footwork must prevent him from slipping on the plate. Much of the footwork depends on arm strength, body physique, location, and type of pitch. The most common footwork techniques are the pivot, jab pivot, and jump pivot (figure 16.10).

b

c

Figure 16.10 Footwork techniques: *(a)* pivot; *(b)* jab pivot; *(c)* jump pivot.

In the pivot, the catcher turns his throwing-side foot after receiving the pitch, loads up, and delivers the ball to the base. For the jab pivot, the catcher takes a short step forward with his throwing-side foot after receiving the pitch. He then turns, loads up, and delivers the ball. In the jump-pivot method, he jumps up after receiving the pitch, aligns his throwing-arm side to the base, loads, and throws the ball.

The key to throwing to any base is to align the directional side to the target. Catchers should work on getting their feet under them so that the upper body is in proper position to throw with the best time, most velocity, and most accuracy.

CATCHER TECHNIQUE DRILLS

Catchers are in full gear for all drills.

Box Throwing Drill

Purpose: To insure proper throwing technique and footwork.

Procedure:
1. A group of four catchers sets up in the outfield in a box pattern, one catcher in each corner. Catchers should be 20 to 30 feet apart.
2. Catcher 1 throws to catcher 2 and so on around the box. Emphasize proper throwing technique and accuracy.

Coaching Points: Grade accuracy and use a stopwatch to time the catcher's throwing speed.

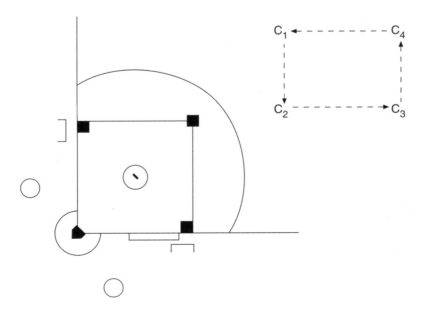

Figure 16.11 Setup for Box Throwing drill.

Box-at-Bases Throwing Drill

Purpose: To insure proper throwing technique and footwork.

Procedure:
1. Four catchers set up in the infield, one catcher at home plate, one at first base, one at second base, and one at third base.
2. Catcher 1 (at home plate) throws to catcher 2 (at first base) and so on around the infield. Emphasize proper throwing technique and accuracy.
3. For variety, have a pitcher pitch from the mound to start the drill.

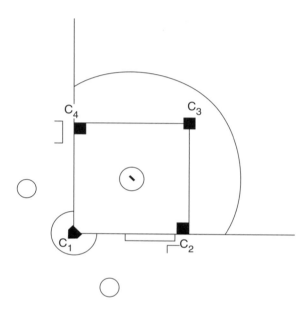

Figure 16.12 Setup for Box-at-Bases Throwing drill.

Second-Base Box Throwing Drill

Purpose: To insure proper throwing technique and footwork.

Procedure:
1. Four catchers set up in the infield, one catcher at home plate, one at first base, one at second base, and one at third base.
2. The coach, standing on the mound, begins the drill by pitching to the catcher at home plate.
3. Catcher 1 (at home plate) throws to catcher 2 (at first base) and so on around the infield. Emphasize proper throwing technique and accuracy.

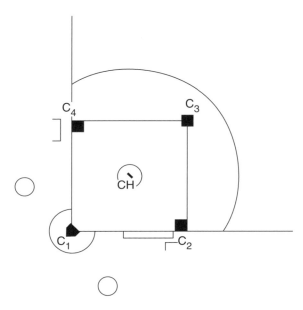

Figure 16.13 Setup for Second-Base Box Throwing drill.

Catcher-in-the-Outfield Throwing Drill

Purpose: To insure proper throwing technique and footwork.

Procedure:

1. Four catchers position themselves in a box shape on the outfield with the coach or a pitcher in the center.

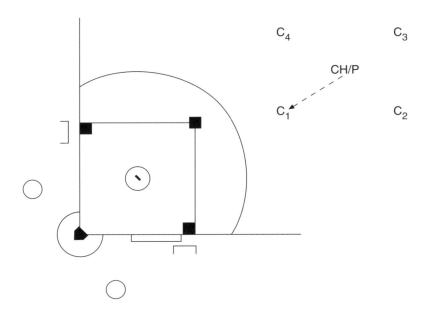

Figure 16.14 Setup for Catcher-in-the-Outfield Throwing drill.

2. The coach or pitcher throws to catcher 1 and calls the base to which the catcher should throw. (The other catchers stand in for the first, second, and third basemen.)

3. The catcher must use the proper footwork to complete the throw to the called base.

Live Drill

Purpose: To insure proper throwing technique and footwork for thwarting steal attempts.

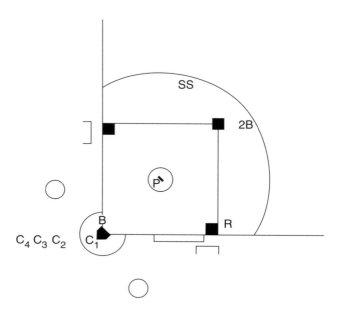

Figure 16.15 Setup for Live drill.

Procedure:
1. Catchers line up behind home plate. The first catcher in line assumes his position behind the plate. A batter steps into the batter's box. The infielders are in position behind the catcher, and a runner is at first base.

2. The pitcher pitches home to start the drill. The runner breaks for second base. The catcher throws to second base to get the runner out.

3. The ball is returned to the pitcher. The pitcher again throws home as the runner breaks for third. The catcher throws to third base to get the runner out.

Coaching Points: Emphasize speed and accuracy.

Catcher's Pick Drill

Purpose: To practice pickoffs of base runners.

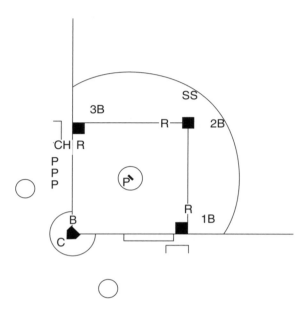

Figure 16.16 Setup for Catcher's Pick drill.

Procedure:

1. The pitcher, catcher, and infielders take their positions on the diamond. Use real batters and base runners or imaginary ones.
2. The catcher or coach signals the pickoff play and the base to which the play is coming.
3. Using any pitch, the pitcher delivers the ball to the catcher, who completes the pickoff play to the specified base.
4. The infielders can continue to drill the rundown off the catcher's pick.

17

Catcher Fielding Plays

The catcher plays a major role in fielding plays. He directs the defense and assumes responsibility in many defensive situations. The catcher not only calls pitches and guides the pitching staff but also communicates with the fielders regarding defensive situations and fielding plays. Through drills and hard work, the catcher can develop all these skills.

FIELDING BUNTS OR TAPPED BALLS

In fielding a ball bunted or tapped in front of the plate, the catcher should try to circle the ball whenever possible. When the ball is rolling away, he puts the glove down to act as a fence and rakes the ball into the glove. He shuffles his feet to get his direction side lined up, creating a throwing lane. The catcher also uses this technique on balls that he blocks on third strikes. He can use an inside or outside throwing lane.

On bunts directly down the third-base line, the catcher should field the ball only when he is 100 percent sure it will stay fair. He gets his chest over the ball and steps over and through. The catcher gloves and secures the ball. The back leg is flexed on the directional side. The lead arm should force the shoulder down, not laterally, so that the ball will stay true in flight and not hit the runner.

MAKING TAG PLAYS AT THE PLATE

To make a tag at home, the catcher must assume the correct setup position. He points his left foot in line with the third-base bag, leaving the back of home plate open, where the runner will slide. The catcher catches and secures the throw. He steps with his foot and shin guard to spin the sliding runner. The catcher tags the runner aggressively (figure 17.1).

When the catcher anticipates contact and the runner tries to bowl him over, the catcher spins with contact to avoid injury.

MAKING FORCE PLAYS AT THE PLATE

On a force play at home (figure 17.2), the catcher stays behind the plate. His feet should feel the back angle of the plate. He reads the direction of the throw and anticipates a bad throw. The catcher understands that home plate is flat and different from a base. He must make sure that the throw does not force him off the plate. He should drag his foot over the plate to complete the play.

On a force play at the plate, we ask our catcher to do two things:

1. alert the umpire that the runner may be running inside the line, and
2. use a full-arm fake to third base if he has no play at first base.

FIELDING POP-UPS

The catcher must understand that the rotation of the pitch causes all pop-ups behind home plate to spin back to the plate. Pop-ups in front of home plate will spin

a

b

c

d

Figure 17.1 The tag play at the plate.

toward the mound. The catcher should catch pop-ups that are spinning back into him.

The catcher holds his mask until he is sure of the trajectory of the ball and then flips the mask away so that no one will trip over it (figure 17.3).

a   b   c

Figure 17.2 The force play at the plate.

BACKING UP BASES

The catcher is the primary backup on balls hit to first base. He sprints at an angle behind the base to field the errant throw.

The catcher will not leave home plate to back up first base when a runner is in scoring position. Some teams have the pitcher rotate to home plate so that the catcher can back up first base.

The catcher also backs up all throws to the infield or pitcher that come from the outfield or from infielders in cut or relay position. He should move in front of home plate and sometimes closer to the mound.

PLAYING PASSED BALLS AND WILD PITCHES

Catchers must work on handling passed balls and wild pitches in drills. Balls toward first base are in the 1,1 zone (figure 17.4). Balls behind home plate are in the 2,2 or back, back zone. Balls in the third-base area are in the 3,3 zone.

The pitcher points to the ball and calls the zone number several times to the catcher. The catcher slides to the ball, rakes it to his glove, and locates the throw to the pitcher covering home plate (figure 17.5).

a

b

c

d

Figure 17.3 The catcher fielding a pop-up.

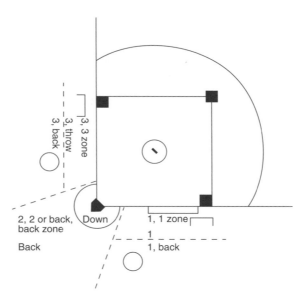

Figure 17.4 Passed-ball and wild-pitch zones.

a

b

Figure 17.5 The catcher fielding a wild pitch or a passed ball.

PITCHOUTS

The pitchout can cause a huge momentum shift in the game. Pitchers and catchers practice pitchouts during bullpen sessions. The catcher steps forward to meet the pitch to reduce the throwing distance. The catcher should work down to up.

INTENTIONAL WALKS

In speed-up baseball rules, intentional walks are obviously not a factor. The catchers may not leave the catcher's box until the pitcher releases the ball. For an intentional walk, the catcher signals the first ball to the pitcher. He flexes his legs, anticipating a bad pitch. The catcher lets the pitcher know that he wants a four-seam fastball. The catcher works down to up.

CATCHER FIELDING DRILLS

Plays-at-the-Plate Fungo Drill

Purpose: To simulate outfield throws to the plate.

Procedure:
1. The catcher assumes his position behind home plate. The coach, with a fungo bat, stands in the outfield, approximately where the center fielder would stand.
2. The coach hits the ball with the fungo bat, simulating an outfield throw to home plate.
3. The catcher practices both force-out plays at the plate and tag plays at the plate.

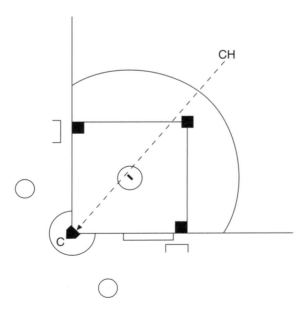

Figure 17.6 Setup for Plays-at-the-Plate Fungo drill.

Plays-at-the-Plate Tackle-Dummy Drill

Purpose: To practice blocking technique.

Procedure:
1. The catcher assumes his position behind home plate. A tackle dummy is positioned on the third-base line.
2. From second base or shortstop, the coach throws the ball to the catcher. The catcher fields the throw then turns to block the tackle dummy.

Coaching Points: Watch for proper blocking technique.

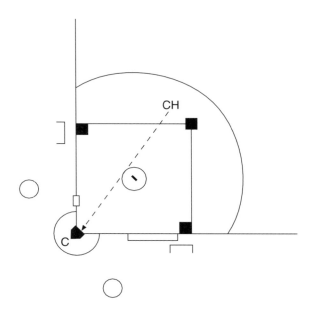

Figure 17.7 Setup for Plays-at-the-Plate Tackle-Dummy drill.

Pop-Up Drill

Purpose: To emphasize proper technique when fielding pop-ups.

Procedure:
1. In the outfield, the catcher assumes the receiving stance.
2. Using a fungo bat, the coach hits a pop-up.
3. The catcher fields the pop-up.

Coaching Points: Emphasize proper technique.

About the American Baseball Coaches Association

The **American Baseball Coaches Association (ABCA)** has undertaken the mission of helping to improve the level of baseball coaching worldwide. The ABCA assists in the promotion of baseball and acts as a sounding board and advocate on issues concerning the various levels of baseball. Furthermore, the ABCA promotes camaraderie and rapport among all baseball coaches, from the amatuer to professional levels. The ABCA also gives recognition to deserving players and coaches through several special sponsorship programs.

The ABCA has more than 5,000 members, including coaches from every state in the country and over 200 international members. Quarterly mailings sent to members each year include newsletters, coaching digests, an ABCA coaches directory, and various website information. Members serve on a variety of committees essential to the functions of the ABCA. An elected executive committee and board of directors govern the ABCA.

The ABCA remains true to the intentions of its founders in its strides to further its members' knowledge and awareness of the game of baseball. The association assists with the development and promotion of the game at all levels. The ABCA's headquarters are located in Mount Pleasant, Michigan.

For more information about the ABCA and the membership opportunities available, visit **www.abca.org**.

About John Winkin

John Winkin served as the coordinator for the *Baseball Skills & Drills* project. Winkin has coached baseball for 42 years in Maine and amassed a 943–670 career record with appearances in 12 NCAA regional tournaments and 6 College World Series. He is a member of the ABCA Coaching Hall of Fame, Maine Baseball Hall of Fame, and the Maine Sports Hall of Fame. Winkin currently has a fellowship in sports leadership at Husson College.

About the Contributors

Three of the most prolific and successful baseball coaches contribute their expertise on behalf of the American Baseball Coaches Association. Each coach has established himself as a top instructor of a specific area of the game.

Courtesy of Texas A & M University

Mark Johnson

Mark Johnson is one of the most respected collegiate coaches in the country and was inducted into the American Baseball Coaches Association Hall of Fame in January 2001.

Since 1985, Johnson has been head coach of the Texas A&M University baseball program, where he has averaged 45 wins a year and ranks among the top 10 winningest coaches in the country. In his 15 seasons, Johnson has a record of 668-279 with three SWC championships, and two Big XII championships. Johnson has led the Aggies to eleven NCAA Regionals and eight times they have reached the Championship Game with two teams advancing to the College World Series. In 1993, the Sporting News selected Johnson as the National Coach of the Year.

Johnson and his wife, Linda, have two sons, both of whom played baseball at Texas A&M and were each awarded the GTE/Texas A&M Male Scholar Athlete of the Year award as seniors. They reside in College Station, Texas.

Courtesy of Clemson University

Jack Leggett

Jack Leggett runs one of the top baseball programs in the country at Clemson University, where he has been head coach since 1994. In his first seven seasons he led Clemson to 339 wins and averaged 48 wins per season—giving him the distinction of having the fifth-winningest program in college baseball. Under Leggett, Clemson has had seven NCAA Tournament berths and three College World Series appearances. In 1994, Coach Leggett had the nation's winningest team with 57 victories in a single season (second in ACC history). He was named ACC Coach of the Year in both 1994 and 1995.

Before taking over the top spot at Clemson, Leggett served as recruiting coordinator and assistant head coach under Bill Wilhelm during the 1992 and 1993 seasons. He was a major contributor to the teams that ranked in the top 20 and advanced to two NCAA regional championships and won the ACC championship in 1993. Leggett has a total of 716 career wins under his belt. He has coached 25 years at the Division I level and 23 as a head coach. At Western Carolina University his teams won 5 straight Southern Conference championships from 1985-1989. He also served as a member of the Division I baseball committee for 5 years.

Leggett has two children, son Tanner and daughter Colby. Leggett resides in Clemson, South Carolina.

Pat McMahon

Pat McMahon was introduced as head baseball coach for the University of Florida in the summer of 2001. Since then, he has gone on to post an 83-40-1 record, earned his 400th collegiate victory, and has coached dozens of Academic All-SEC players. He arrived at Florida after serving four years as the head baseball coach at Missis-sippi State University teams where his teams consistently ranked at the top of the Southeastern Conference (SEC) and in the top 25 nationally. McMahon became only the second coach in the SEC's history to take a team to the College World Series in his first season.

In 2001, McMahon earned USA Baseball's National Coach of the Year honors and in 1998 the American Baseball Coaches Association (ABCA) selected him as the South Region Coach of the Year. In 1994, McMahon was designated the Coach of the Year for both the Colonial Athletic Association and the state of Virginia.

Coaching on a variety of levels since 1976 at Florida, Mississippi State University and Old Dominion, Coach McMahon has developed a host of players who went on to success in major league baseball, including Jeff Brantley, Will Clark, Rafael Palmeiro, and Bobby Thigpen.

McMahon and his wife, Cheri, have two children, daughter Logan and son J. Wells. McMahon and his family live in "Gator Country".

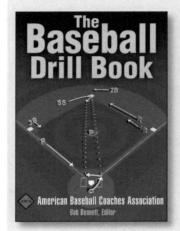

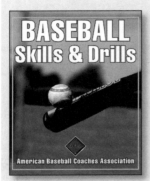